Lacock
Chippenham
Wiltshire

A Magna Field Guide

AMPHIBIANS
AND REPTILES

A Magna Field Guide

AMPHIBIANS AND REPTILES

By Jiří Čihař

Illustrated by Alena Čepická

Text by Jiří Čihař
Translated by Marie Hejlová
Illustrated by Alena Čepická
Graphic design by Soňa Valoušková

This English edition published 1994 by
Harveys Bookshop Ltd.
Magna Road, Wingston, Leicester LE8 2ZH,
and produced in co-operation with Arcturus
Publishing Limited

© 1990 Aventinum, Prague
First published 1979 by Artia, Prague

ISBN 1-85422-788-2
Printed in the Czech Republic
3/10/19/51-02

CONTENTS

INTRODUCTION

Keeping a vivarium as a hobby has recently become more and more popular. Of the animals kept in vivaria the best known are undoubtedly the amphibians and reptiles. Their behaviour, reproduction, development and growth have been closely observed in laboratories and recently published work has contributed to a deeper understanding of many biological principles.

Of course, the study of animals in captivity—even if it produces valuable information and enlarges our present knowledge—cannot replace observation of animals in their natural environment. Here, their behaviour is not limited or affected by space factors or the care of the keeper; each animal has to compete with others and survive among many enemies. It is only through exhaustive research into the ethology of animals that we will reach a clear and comprehensive view of the function and significance of the biosphere—a complex which includes man as an important component.

The growth of human civilization has had an unfavourable effect on nature as a whole, including the distribution and numbers of small vertebrates such as newts, salamanders, frogs, lizards and snakes. These animals are disappearing at an alarmingly rapid rate, or have faded out altogether from places where they lived in abundance only a few years ago. From time immemorial, man has persecuted amphibians and reptiles, even more than other animals, through superstition, repugnance and fear.

Modern times bring another danger. In many places man has substantially violated the natural environment of small vertebrates: by drying up swamps and pools, draining soggy meadows, regulating rivers and brooks, using newly developed pesticides in soil cultivation and by polluting water and air with waste from industry and big cities. In this way he has jeopardized the existence of many animal species, including amphibians and reptiles, or exterminated them altogether. Still worse is the position of species from which man draws direct profit and which, for this very reason, he intensively and often imprudently hunts: some species of frogs for their legs, crocodiles, monitor lizards and big snakes for their skins, certain species of turtles for their meat, eggs and tortoise-shell. This being so, it is high time to include such directly endangered species on the list of strictly protected animals.

A great many people still regard newts, salamanders, frogs, lizards and snakes as having no value or even as explicitly harmful animals. However, anyone who becomes more closely acquainted with the way of life and significance of amphibians and reptiles in the balance of nature is bound fundamentally to change his point of view. This is one of the aims of this book. It will acquaint all those who are interested in nature with the fascinating and varied European amphibians and reptiles as well as some of their exotic relations and with their biology, distribution and classification. It is only detailed knowledge and understanding of these small animals that can ultimately induce people to protect them.

In its introductory part, the book acquaints the reader with the most important amphibians and reptiles of the world and presents some interesting details of their biology. The illustrated part of the book includes detailed descriptions of the way of life of individual European species, of their distribution, occurrence, food, breeding habits, and the most important living conditions which must be provided if they are to be kept successfully in captivity.

AMPHIBIANS

Amphibians are the first animals which, in prehistoric times (350—380 million years ago), emerged from their aquatic environment to become land-dwellers for a substantial part of their lives. They represent a transitional stage from fishes to higher vertebrates—reptiles, birds and mammals, and probably developed from primitive lobe-finned fish (Crossopterygii). The ancestors of the present-day forms of amphibians lived as early as the Jurassic.

Modern members of the class Amphibia can be divided into three large groups or orders according to the shape of the body. The first of these, the order Caecilia, consists of limbless animals which live most of their lives in obscurity underground; it includes more than 150 species that inhabit the tropics and resemble large annelid worms. The second order, the Urodela or tailed amphibians, comprises about 150 species of salamanders, newts, giant salamanders and axolotls. The largest group is the order Anura, which includes approximately 2,000 species. These are frogs having no tail in their adult stage—true frogs (Ranidae), tree frogs (Hylidae), clawed frogs (Xenopidae), tongueless frogs (Pipidae), toads (Bufonidae), spadefoots (Pelobatidae), fire-bellies and midwife toads (Discoglossidae), and several other families.

Amphibians inhabit all geographical zones, with the exception of the Antarctic and the northernmost regions beyond the Arctic Circle. Most species live in tropical and subtropical regions, their numbers rapidly decreasing towards the poles. They are also sparsely represented in high-lying mountainous districts. Their natural habitat is both water and dry land; but there are amphibians who spend the greater part of their lives in trees, particularly in the tropical countries. Several other

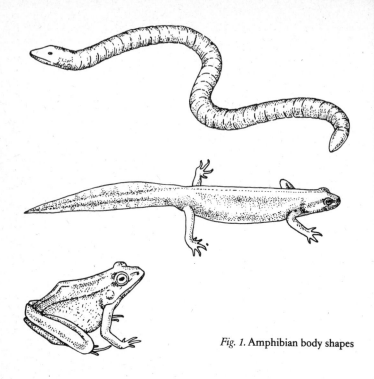

Fig. 1. Amphibian body shapes

species have become quite well adapted to life in arid steppes and deserts, in places with only a trace of water. With the exception of the Argentinian toad *Bufo arenarum* and the Californian *Bufo boreas halophilus,* modern amphibians, unlike some of their extinct ancestors, cannot tolerate salt water.

All amphibians have a variable body temperature which fluctuates with the temperature of their surroundings. Their skin is, for the most part, bare and glandular. Multicellular glands contained in the skin protect the animals from desiccation, and, in many cases, exude poisonous secretions as a defense mechanism—this applies particularly to terrestrial species. Periodically, salamanders and frogs shed the outermost layer of their skin—the former in one piece, the latter in smaller patches. In many species, pigment cells in the underlayers of the skin bring about conspicuous colour changes. The skin of the aquatic larvae of amphibians contains numerous sensory cells, usually thickly clustered on the head and sides, which serve — like the lateral line in fishes — as a long-range tactile-sense organ.

The spinal skeleton of the amphibians consists of the cervical, thoracic, sacral and caudal vertebrae. Two joints connect the cervical part to a flat, barely movable skull. The number of vertebrae varies: frogs have nine, caecilians sometimes more than a hundred. The thorax of amphibians is undeveloped and the skeletal system of the fore limbs is not joined to the thoracic vertebrae.

Sight is the most important sense for the majority of amphibians and the well-developed eyes have mobile protective eyelids. Only amphibians living permanently in subterranean waters or in the ground have rudimentary or underdeveloped

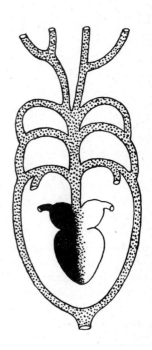

Fig. 2. Blood circulation in amphibians

sight organs. The shape of the pupil is characteristic of individual groups (toads, spadefoots, etc.), and represents an important distinguishing feature. Hearing is well developed, particularly in adult frogs which communicate with each other in the breeding season by calling or croaking. Resonance organs located either at mouth corners or on the throat amplify the volume of sound. The sense of smell, being of major importance only in the aquatic forms and in the tadpoles of frogs, is relatively poorly developed in adult frogs.

In their larval stage, all amphibians breathe through gills; it is only the forms that live in water all their life that have retained gills in their adult stage. In terrestrial species, gills disappear by the end of the larval stage and lungs start developing. However, a considerable part of the animal's oxygen consumption is made up by cutaneous respiration — that is, through the skin. This is why the skin of amphibians is thickly interwoven with a network of fine blood capillaries across which gas exchange takes place.

The amphibian heart has two distinctly separated auricles and one muscular ventricle, which circulates mixed arterial and venous blood in vessels throughout the body.

The mouth cavity of amphibians contains small horny teeth and a tongue which may be flicked forwards in some species but is firmly attached in others; still other groups, however, have no tongue at all. Digestion takes place in the gullet, the stomach and the intestines which terminate in the cloaca. The larvae of amphibians mostly live on a vegetarian diet but in adult amphibians this is replaced by animal food, particularly insects.

With a few exceptions, the two sexes of amphibians are recognizably different. In the breeding season, males sometimes develop particularly conspicuous secondary sexual features: for example, powerful skin crests in newts or swellings on the thumbs of frogs' fore limbs.

The fertilization of eggs is usually external, as in fish, occurring at the moment of laying by the female. In some groups, for example in salamanders, eggs are fertilized in the female's oviducts. Amphibians lay their eggs either singly, in long strings or in clusters. Most amphibians are oviparous — that is, they lay eggs — but some groups do not lay their eggs until the embryos have become fully developed larvae. Such a phenomenon is known as pseudoviviparity or ovoviviparity. Large-headed larvae with bushy external gills hatch from the eggs. They move about using their tails, cling to plants by help of special adhesive organs and live on plant or animal food. They grow and undergo a number of substantial external and internal changes: progressively the limbs increase in size, the lungs develop, adhesive organs disappear and, depending on the species, the tail becomes stunted and the gills are gradually absorbed. This complex transformation of the larva into a mature animal is governed by a hormone produced by the thyroid gland and is called metamorphosis. It is characteristic of some amphibian species (olms, axolotls) that metamorphosis fails to take place and the animal remains in the larval stage throughout its life; in this stage it is also capable of producing offspring. This phenomenon is called neoteny.

Because the body temperature of amphibians varies with the temperature of their surroundings, they spend the unfavourable cold season of the year in a variety of shelters, or in water, in a state of winter sleep or hibernation. During this time, all life processes are reduced to the minimum. In the temperate zones, it is only when the temperature rises in the spring that amphibians begin to leave their winter shelters to resume their active life.

Caecilians

At first sight we would not class the caecilians among amphibians. They resemble large annelid worms: their long, snake-like body seems to be made up of a large number of segments but, of course, the similarity to worms is only superficial. They possess, as do all amphibians, a spine and a skull attached to it. Their limbs, however, have not developed, nor can their remnants be found on the skeleton.

Caecilians are distributed throughout the tropical and subtropical zone of Asia, Africa and America. With only a few exceptions, the adults live underground where they burrow deep passages and forage for their food.

The skin of caecilians is soft and moist like that of other amphibians. In most cases, however, it is found to contain tiny osseous scales; these probably represent the last remnants of osseous scales which covered the skin of Stegocephali — tailed amphibians that lived in great abundance in seas of the Carboniferous period. This indicates that, from the evolutionary point of view, caecilians are a very ancient group.

Adult caecilians have small eyes often concealed by skin or even embedded in the skull. To find their way in the permanent darkness of underground passages, they have developed short tactile antennae that can be extended and retracted; these are located between eyes and nostrils.

The largest caecilians — for example, the Columbian *Caecilia thompsoni* — attain a length of more than 1.5 metres, while the smallest ones are only a few centimetres long. Some species are viviparous, others lay relatively large eggs. Females frequently coil their bodies round their clutches and take care of them underground until they hatch. In this way a suitably moist environment for the eggs is maintained. With the exception of *Rhinatrema,* which passes through a larval stage characterized by external gills, both viviparous and oviparous caecilian young hatch as perfect replicas of the adult animals. Though they are of great interest, much remains to be discovered about these peculiar, primitive amphibians.

Giant Salamanders, Axolotls and Lungless Salamanders

These belong to the group of tailed amphibians having an elongate, cylindrical body with a clearly distinct head, four limbs and a tail which the animal retains throughout its life. Giant salamanders (family Cryptobranchidae) inhabit fresh waters of south-eastern Asia and North America. The largest species of this group attain the impressive length of 1.5 metres. Their large and powerfully built body is borne by relatively feeble, small legs which would be of little use on dry land. All of them breathe by means of gills in the larval stage and by means of both lungs and gills in the adult stage, the lungs then playing the greater part.

The Japanese Giant Salamander *(Megalobatrachus japonicus)* is the largest species in the family; it grows to about 1.5 metres long and lives in clean streams on the Japanese islands. Although it never leaves water, it has to come to the surface every 6 to 10 minutes to breathe. It captures fish and frogs by a swift sideward movement of the head and gulps down its prey whole. Although its eyes are relatively small (only about 4 mm in diameter) it sees very well at short distances. It breeds in August or September when the female lays a huge number of minute pink eggs joined in a string. After fertilizing the eggs, the male keeps guard over them until the small larvae hatch out.

The mountain streams of China are inhabited by the related Chinese Giant Salamander *(Megalobatrachus davidianus)* which attains a length of about 1.2 metres. North America is the home of the Hellbender *(Cryptobranchus alleganiensis)* which grows to about 75 cm in length. The female Hellbender fastens her eggs to stones to prevent the rushing mountain rivers from washing them away. After hatching, the larvae travel upstream in rivers and brooks.

Closely related to the giant salamanders are the North American axolotls of the family Ambystomatidae. Their larvae have large, branched external gills on either side of the head. It is typical of some species that metamorphosis fails to take place and the animal is capable of breeding in its larval stage. In the case of the Mexican Axolotl *(Ambystoma mexicanum)* it was found that whenever the water-level in an artificial tank was lowered, the external gills degenerated and the larvae developed into lung-breathing animals. Under natural conditions, this is a reaction to drying-up of the water. If the water-level remains constant, the animals do not undergo metamorphosis and attain maturity in their larval stage.

The giant among axolotls is the Tiger Salamander *(Ambysto-*

ma tigrinum) which lives in North American lowland waters from Long Island down to Florida, and reaches a length of 30 cm. In the western parts of the USA it lives in the neotenic form only, while in the east its larvae metamorphose several months after the eggs have been laid; their gills are absorbed and the adults become land-dwellers. In this case metamorphosis is stimulated by a higher content of iodine in water.

Closely allied to axolotls is the large family of lungless salamanders (Plethodontidae), distributed throughout Asia and America. Having no lungs, the plethodonts breathe through the skin and the mucous membrane in their mouths. A single species only, *Hydromantes genei,* occurs in Europe. Two species of lungless salamanders from North America are most interesting: the first of these, the Texas Blind Salamander *(Typhlomolge rathbuni),* inhabits underground waters and artesian wells; its eyes are hidden deep under the skin and its large external gills serve throughout its life as a breathing organ. It has long and extremely slender legs. A further interesting plethodont is *Aneides lugubris,* an arboreal salamander from the western coast of North America. Like all plethodonts it has no lungs, nor does it have gills. It breathes through the entire surface of its body (cutaneous respiration); the skin covering the tips of its digits is richly supplied with blood sinuses which probably function as a substitute for external gills. It is also well known for its ability to produce sounds—a soft but clearly audible chirping.

Salamanders and Newts

The most numerous family of urodelan amphibians is the family Salamandridae, which includes salamanders and newts. The two groups are anatomically similar but their ways of life are substantially different. Adult salamanders are predominantly terrestrial animals but always keep along the water's edge or in damp places. The tail is circular in cross-section. Newts, on the other hand, spend the greater part of their lives

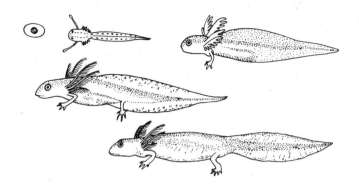

Fig. 3. Larval development of the newt

in water, even in their adult stage, and the tail, which is used in swimming, is deep and laterally flattened.

Whereas salamanders are viviparous and mate on dry land, all newts breed in water, where they have a specific way of mating: the male deposits capsules containing spermatozoa (spermatophores) on the bottom and the female then picks them up and places them in her cloaca. Subsequently she lays fertilized eggs into the water, and these hatch as larvae which resemble the small, slender tadpoles of frogs.

Newts have a remarkable capacity of regeneration and can replace some lost or damaged parts of the body. Not only a wounded or completely torn-off tail but whole limbs, and even injured parts of the eye, can grow again.

Fire-bellies, Midwife Toads, Tongueless Frogs and Clawed Frogs

From salamanders and newts we come to the anurans or tail-less amphibians. These animals have in their adult stage a short, tailless body, short fore limbs with four toes and long-er hind limbs with five toes. They have large subcutaneous cavities filled with a body fluid—the lymph.

The Old-World family Discoglossidae includes stout, short-legged frogs whose skin in covered with horny tubercles. They have a disc-like tongue which is firmly attached to the floor of the mouth and therefore cannot flick out to catch the prey. This family includes fire-bellies of the genus *Bombina,* mid-wife toads of the genus *Alytes* and frogs of the genus *Discoglos-sus.* Some European representatives of this family are dealt with in the illustrated section of this book.

In Africa and America there occur interesting tongueless and clawed species in the family Pipidae. They spend the greater part of their lives in water. The largest is the South American Surinam Toad *(Pipa pipa)* which may reach a length of 25 cm. It is known from the tropical regions of Brazil and Guyana where it inhabits waters densely overgrown with aquatic vegetation. On the digits of its fore legs the Su-rinam Toad has peculiar star-shaped excrescences which it uses when foraging for its prey at the bottom.

The breeding behaviour of this species is quite remarkable. When the male has enticed the female by uttering a series of loud, metallic clicks, he embraces her body from above with his fore legs, and presses her tubular, protruding oviduct against her back, thus helping to expel the eggs which he simultaneously fertilizes. He then presses each egg into the thickened skin of the female's back. When about 60 eggs have been placed there, the skin swells still more to encase them so that each egg has its own little 'chamber' where it continues to develop in relative safety. Thus it is on the female's back that the embryos develop, the tadpoles hatch and even their meta-morphosis takes place. All this time, the mother nourishes her

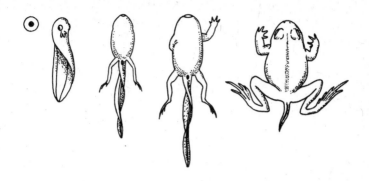

Fig. 4. Larval development of the frog

offspring with a secretion produced by her skin. The young leave their pockets on their mother's back as miniature versions of the adults.

One of the African representatives of the family Pipidae is the Platanna *(Xenopus laevis)*. All its features point to the fact that it is exclusively aquatic. Its protruding eyes are situated on the top of the head and its long and powerful hind legs end in broadly webbed toes. The fore legs are short and equipped with three little hooked claws used by the frog in foraging for food.

In the periods of drought, South African waters inhabited by clawed frogs regularly dry up. When this happens the frogs burrow deep into the mud to wait in a sort of summer sleep (aestivation) until the unfavourable period is over and the water soaks through the mud again, opening their way out. The clawed frog larvae differ conspicuously from the tadpoles of other frogs: they have a wide mouth with long whiskers at the corners and look rather like small catfish. Clawed frogs are important to man in his fight against malaria since their main food is the larvae of the mosquitoes which transmit this tropical disease.

Spadefoots, Leptodactylids and Horned Frogs

The next frog family, the spadefoots (Pelobatidae), have hind limbs adapted to burrowing, often bearing large horny projections. Unlike other frogs, they have vertically contracting pupils and perhaps their most conspicuous anatomical feature is the absence of ribs. They are distributed over Europe, northeastern Africa, southern Asia and North America.

In southern Asia, spadefoots of the genus *Megophrys* are very abundant. One of these, *Megophrys montana,* has an interesting habit: it swims in water in an upright, vertical position, using its broad mouth to collect insects and other animals floating on the surface. Some frogs of this genus are fearless creatures: if exposed to danger, they open their jaws wide, raise themselves up and, uttering loud croaking sounds, pounce upon the enemy, even on man.

The most numerous representatives of the American spadefoots are frogs of the genus *Scaphiopus* whose skin produces a burning, putridly smelling exudation. Because the puddles inhabited by these frogs dry up very quickly, their breeding biology is adapted to these extreme conditions. On the evening after the puddles are filled with rain water, a mass mating of frogs takes place. Their eggs and tadpoles take a very short time to develop and young froglets are often capable of leaving water after only twelve days. The tadpoles of other species in the genus burrow deep into the mud to survive the period of drought.

Frogs of the family Leptodactylidae are distributed throughout the tropical zone of both the Old and the New World and Australia. The males produce a piercing, piping sound. Some of them, such as *Leptodactylus pentadactylus,* are among the largest frogs, often exceeding 20 cm in length.

Another leptodactylid, *Cyclorana platycephala,* lives in the arid regions of central Australia. In the rainy season it accumulates so much water in its body that it resembles a large ball. When the dry season begins, it burrows deep into the ground where it stays until the end of the unfavourable weather. The aborigines know it very well and, at times of greatest water shortage, dig out these living reservoirs and suck the water out of them.

The South American horned frogs (genus *Ceratophrys*) well deserve their name: their upper eyelids are elongated to form short, pointed horns. They include huge frogs almost 30 cm in length. Their food consists not only of various invertebrates but also of smaller vertebrates.

Toads and Atelopids

Toads (family Bufonidae) are found in the temperate and the tropical zone all over the world, excepting the Australian region, Madagascar and some of the smaller Pacific islands. Most of them live in tropical and subtropical areas. There are some 13 species in North America and three in Europe.

Their stout body is covered by a warty skin; they have toothless mandibles and short limbs, and are very slow in movement. If attacked, they emit poisonous secretions from venom glands located behind their head; in some species, these secretions are extremely effective — the most virulent poison is exuded by the toad *Bufo alvarius* from the Colorado River basin.

Toads are most useful: they feed chiefly on insects, and in gardens they help to control slugs. This is why some of them, for example the South American marine toad *(Bufo marinus)*, which reaches a length of about 25 cm, are intentionally introduced to sugar-cane plantations in order to help man in his fight against injurious pests.

In comparison with this giant toad, the South American mountain toad *Bufo rosei*, Rose's Toad, is a dwarf: when fully grown, it measures only 2 cm. The newly metamorphosed froglets of this species are as small as a wheat grain.

The Vaquero *(Rhinoderma darwini*, family Rhinodermatidae), from the coastal forests of Argentina and Chile, is unique in its breeding habits. At breeding time, several males gather near the deposited eggs, waiting for the young tadpoles to emerge. Then each male swallows five to fifteen larvae into his vocal pouch where he carries them until the tadpoles complete their metamorphosis. This way of looking after the young is analogous to that known to us from other animal classes: similar care of offspring is demonstrated by fish in the genera *Tilapia* and *Haplochromis.*

Tree Frogs

Tree frogs (Hylidae) are, as a rule, small, slender and very brightly coloured frogs, outstandingly adapted for arboreal life. The tips of their toes are provided with suctorial pads or discs enabling them to climb trees and cling firmly to leaves. They spend most of their lives on trees and bushes, returning to water only to mate. The following tree frogs are listed among the largest: *Hyla dolichopsis* from New Guinea, the Giant Tree Frog *(Hyla maxima)* from South America, and the Cuban Tree Frog *(Osteopilus septentrionalis),* the last one attaining a length of 14 cm. Most tree frogs live in the tropics and subtropics, and only a few species are found in colder regions.

Some tree frogs have interesting ways of protecting their young. For instance, the female Goeldi's Frog *(Hyla [Flectonotus] goeldi)* from South America carries the whole clutch of eggs as well as the larvae on her back between two skin folds. In shallows at the edge of moorlands and pools, the Giant Tree Frog *(Hyla maxima)* from South America builds small circular ponds, protected from all sides by small mud dykes. In building the dykes and deepening the ponds, it uses its fore limbs whose dilated fingers serve as a trowel for smoothing the earth. The ponds are about 30 cm across and the dyke may be as much as 10 cm high. These enclosed pools protect the Giant Tree Frog's offspring against all enemies that could jeopardize them in open water. Still other tree frogs lay their eggs on leaves bending over the water. When the tadpoles hatch, they fall directly into the water where their subsequent development continues in the usual way.

True Frogs

The family of true frogs (Ranidae), containing a multitude of species, can be found almost all over the world. True frogs are amply represented even in the European fauna. They mostly live close to water but some species may be found in woods, in meadows, or even in tree-tops. These frogs have markedly long hind limbs, tiny teeth in the upper jaw and a projectile tongue which is flicked out to seize small insects and other invertebrates. Large members of this family are able to catch even small reptiles, birds, mammals and fish. They themselves are a much sought after prey for a number of other animals: mammals and birds, numerous fish, turtles and snakes. With so many predators, true frogs need to be extremely prolific: one female can lay about 5,000 eggs in one season.

True frogs usually do not care for the young but an exception is the Chinese frog *Rana adenopleura* which builds little pools along the banks of brooks and rivers similar to those built by the Giant Tree Frog. Its ponds are, however, much more simple.

The largest of the true frogs, and also the largest frog in the world, is the African Goliath Frog *(Gigantorana goliath)*. It can attain a length of over 40 cm and can weigh as much as 6 kg. It inhabits deep pools in rapidly flowing rivers of south-western Cameroon, Gabon and Angola, and is extremely shy. The giant among North American frogs is the Bull Frog *(Rana catesbeiana)* which may grow to 25 cm in length. The booming sounds made by this frog actually suggest the mooing of cattle.

The Hairy Frog *Astylosternus robustus* from western Africa presents an odd appearance, particularly in the breeding season. It is unique amongst amphibians in that from its sides and hind limbs grow long, fine filaments which superficially resemble mammalian hair. Anatomically, of course, these filaments have nothing in common with hair. Their actual purpose has not yet been fully ascertained. The fact that they are richly interwoven with minute blood vessels leads some zoologists to believe that they serve as an additional respiratory organ. On the other hand, there are some who consider these structures to be of significance in helping individuals of each sex to make contact during the mating season. Significantly these filaments are longest in the breeding season when they measure about 1.5 cm.

REPTILES

The class Reptilia is of ancient origin. It reached its golden age in the Mesozoic era, during the Jurassic and the Cretaceous period, which — for good reasons — is referred to as the Age of Reptiles. At that time, gigantic predatory and herbivorous dinosaurs (*Plesiosaurus, Tyrannosaurus, Ichthyosaurus, Placodon, Brontosaurus, Pterodactylus* and many others) as well as a vast multitude of smaller reptiles maintained their dominance of the land, water and air. The dinosaurs died out by the end of the Cretaceous period; smaller and more adaptive reptiles, however, went on developing and gave rise to present-day lizards and snakes.

The reptiles of today, comprising almost 6,000 known species, are divided into four orders. The first of these, the Rhynchocephalia, are all extinct except a single species — the New-Zealand Tuatara *(Sphenodon punctatus)*. This is a very ancient reptile resembling a big lizard. The second order — the Chelonia — includes the turtles and tortoises, peculiar reptiles whose short and massive body is covered by an osseous shell. The order of crocodiles (Crocodylia) includes large-sized reptiles adapted to life in water and having long, powerfully toothed jaws, an elongate body and a powerful tail. The last and most numerous order of living reptiles is the Squamata which includes more than 95 per cent of all reptiles; these are classed into two suborders — Lacertilia (geckos, iguanas, lizards etc.) and Ophidia (snakes).

Reptiles are mostly land-dwellers and their body is covered by a horny skin which protects them from desiccation. In contrast to fishes and amphibians, they are no longer dependent on the aquatic environment, not even during their developmental stages; their embryos develop within egg mem-

Fig. 5. Reptile body shapes

branes, protected by a leathery or calcareous shell. Throughout their lives, reptiles breathe by means of lungs. Their heart has two auricles, and a ventricle which is divided by a more or less complete partition into right and left chambers. This implies that, unlike the condition in amphibians, deoxygenated blood is more completely separated from oxygenated blood. Although the body temperature of reptiles is still variable and dependent upon the temperature of the surrounding environment, some groups do show some indication of thermoregulation. Most species live in the tropics and subtropics and they rapidly decrease in number towards both poles.

Some reptiles reach a relatively old age. Best known in this respect are probably chelonians. It has been proved that the Spur-thighed Tortoise *(Testudo graeca)* from south-east Europe can attain the age of 100 years; the life span of Giant

Tortoises *(Testudo gigantea)* from the Galápagos Islands can even exceed 200 years.

Reptiles are found in a large variety of habitats. They are abundant on land, numerous species live in trees and some have become secondarily adapted to life in fresh- or salt-water. A number of reptiles spend most of their life underground.

Reptiles are either carnivorous or herbivorous. Some of them have a very specific diet—the well-known African snake *Dasypeltis scabra,* for example, feeds exclusively on birds' eggs. Carnivorous reptiles usually catch their prey by surprisingly quick assaults. Many have teeth, others, for example turtles, are toothless. The salivary glands of venomous snakes have become partially modified into venom glands. Special teeth are used to inject the venom into the prey's body. These venom-conducting fangs are often hollow or have a deep groove running along their length through which the venom is introduced into the wound. Snake venom affects the central ner-

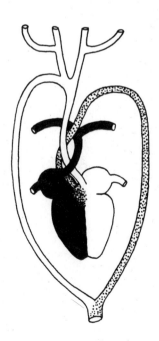

Fig. 6. Blood circulation in reptiles

vous system, damages blood vessel walls, decomposes and destroys both red and white blood cells, and causes blood coagulation inside the vessels. It is predominantly composed of proteins, such as albumin, globulin, mucin and peptone.

In most reptiles, sight is the most important sense, but some subterranean species often have reduced eyes. Organs of hearing are poorly developed in some groups, whilst in others they are extremely well developed. Most reptiles are endowed with complex organs of smell and taste, for example Jacobson's organ which is situated in the roof of the mouth, and which, through the mediation of the tongue tip, perceives both smells and tastes. Some snakes (rattle-snakes and boas) have special thermal receptors on their head enabling them to perceive the whereabouts of warm-blooded animals.

The skeleton of reptiles varies widely throughout the various groups; in all cases, however, it is almost entirely ossified. The skull is attached to the spine by means of a single articular area or condyle. The number of spinal vertebrae varies considerably, ranging from 30 to more than 700. Reptiles have well developed ribs: in some groups (crocodiles and tuataras) not only thoracic but also abdominal ribs are present.

Reptiles never have gills and always breathe by means of lungs. In snakes, the left lung is either absent or, as in the Boidae, substantially smaller than the right lung, which is greatly elongated.

The sex of all reptiles is clearly differentiated, some of them displaying a marked sexual dimorphism. Fertilization is internal, and development is direct—without metamorphosis.

In the temperate and cold zones, reptiles survive the winter period in hibernation, remaining in an entirely motionless state. Their breathing and heart-beat are almost imperceptible. Hibernation may last 6—8 months or more. The temperature of the environment in winter shelters is usually between 1 and 3° C. During the hibernation period, a number of reptiles of the same species often share a single shelter.

Tuatara

The Tuatara *(Sphenodon punctatus)* of New Zealand, which resembles a large lizard, is the only living representative of the order Rhynchocephalia. It is often referred to as a living fossil as it is the only reptile to have survived from the Triassic and Jurassic to the present day. In those remote periods, about 170 million years ago, there were many species of rhynchocephalians, some of which lived in Europe, Asia, South America and South Africa.

Today the Tuatara inhabits only 20 small, waterless islets adjacent to New Zealand where it is not threatened by introduced wild pigs, mice and rats. These alien species exterminated the Tuatara on all the islands on which man had settled. At present the Tuatara is included with the most strictly protected animals.

The Tuatara attains a length of about 70 cm, males being slightly larger than females. The males also have a more prominent crest on their head and back. The skin colour ranges from olive-green to brownish with yellow spots.

The Tuatara differs from all the other reptiles in its antomical structure. Its spine is formed of primitive biconcave vertebrae and, on the dorsal part of the ribs, there are short, hook-like projections pointing backwards. Like crocodiles, it has

Fig. 7. Tuatara

preserved its abdominal ribs which are a remnant of the original plastron of primeval amphibians—the long extinct Stegocephali. The most conspicuous feature of the skull is a circular opening between the parietal bones — the site of the parietal third eye. In young individuals this can be easily distinguished as it is covered by a translucent scale. In adult animals the skin covering becomes so thick that it is unlikely to let any light pass through it. Thus the Tuatara's 'third eye' has no auxiliary visual function. This interesting organ is a remnant of a secondary organ of sight which, in extinct forms of reptiles, was situated on the vertex.

The Tuataras' eyes resemble those of lizards. However, besides the lower and the upper eyelid, there is a third one — the nictitating membrane. The teeth are set along the edges of the jaws and are permanent. A characteristic feature of the Tuatara which distinguishes it from other reptiles is the absence of any external copulatory organ in the male.

There is an interesting co-existence with petrels—birds nesting in underground burrows which are often shared by the Tuataras. Sometimes, however, they excavate their own. These they leave for a short time in the morning and late in the afternoon to bask in the sun. They hunt for food only by night. They gather insects, molluscs and worms but occasionally also capture young birds, small snakes, lizards and geckos. They hibernate in their burrows and do not leave them before August when the New Zealand spring sets in.

Between October and December, females lay 8—14 eggs into shallow excavations in the ground which they cover with grass, leaves and soil. The development of embryos inside the eggs takes a whole year and the young do not hatch until the following spring. They break the egg shell using a special 'egg tooth'—a horny projection at the end of the snout which disappears approximately one week after hatching.

Turtles, Tortoises and Terrapins

These reptiles belong to the Chelonia—a very ancient group, which is represented today by more than two hundred species.

One of their characteristics is the bony shell which protects the internal organs. This serves as an effective safeguard against enemies as many species are capable of withdrawing their head, tail and legs into the shell. Strong scales covering the legs are all that remains visible. Some species are even capable of sealing both the front and the rear openings of the shell by tilting the mobile lower part of the plastron upwards. The shell of chelonians consists of an upper part (carapace) and a lower part (plastron) which are either fused together or connected by means of a flexible ligament. The shell is formed of bony shields covered from above by horny plates or coated with a thick layer of soft skin. The skull bones are also very strong. Chelonians' jaws are toothless, covered by a horny tissue; the fleshy tongue is firmly attached to the base of the mouth cavity.

Many members of the group live on dry land, others inhabit fresh waters, still others are sea-dwellers. Their eggs, however, are always laid exclusively on dry land—in sand or in soil.

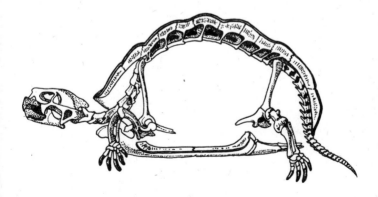

Fig. 8. Skeletal structure of a chelonian

Terrestrial species are predominantly herbivorous, while those which live in water are mostly carnivorous.

The chelonians include both small-sized species only a few centimetres long and very large ones such as the Giant Leatherback Turtle *(Dermochelys coriacea)* which approaches a length of 3 metres and can weigh up to a ton. The largest terrestrial species are the Elephantine Tortoise *(Testudo elephantopus)* which lives on the Galápagos Islands and the Giant Tortoise *(Testudo gigantea)* from the Seychelles. These giant species were still abundant in the middle of the last century. Since that time, however, their numbers have continuously decreased due to the fact that, weighing as much as 250 kg, they represented a welcome supply of fresh food for whaler crews on their long voyages. The people who colonized these islands brought with them dogs, cats, pigs, mice and rats— alien animals with which the indigenous reptiles were unadapted to compete. Even now, these introduced animals continue to destroy the tortoises' eggs and young.

The snake-necked freshwater turtles in the family Chelidae are particularly interesting. The best known of these is the South American Matamata *(Chelys fimbriatus)*. Its head is elongated into a long snout. Its colour provides an excellent camouflage among stones on the bottom of rivers and brooks. Its mouth is very large—this is associated with the peculiar way of capturing food: when the prey approaches, the turtle opens its huge mouth and a fish, frog, or a similar mouthful is sucked in with the inrush of water. Most of the time it lies quietly at the bottom of shallow waters with only its small tubular proboscis jutting above the surface and acting as a snorkel.

Alligators, Crocodiles and Gavials

All the representatives of the order which contains the crocodiles (Crocodylia) have a heavily built body with an elongate head, a strong, laterally flattened tail and powerful legs. The shorter fore legs have five digits and the bulkier hind legs have only four, interconnected with a web. The skin of crocodiles and their relatives is covered with strong, scaly armour underlain by bony plates. The elongate snout contains conical, sharp teeth that are not rooted in the jaws but only seated in cavities (alveoli). Crocodiles inhabit the banks of tropical and subtropical rivers, lakes and swamps, yet they spend the greater part of their lives in water. Some of them may live in brackish waters and even swim across sea straits. All crocodilians lay eggs with a hard, porous shell; they cover them up with sand or build special nests of leaves and twigs.

Crocodiles, alligators and gavials swim in water with the help of their tail, holding their legs close to the body. They are quick and strong swimmers. When out of water, they usually lie on their bellies but sometimes they rest in an upright position, supported by their fore legs. Both their larynx and pharynx can be tightly closed by the broad tongue, and this enables them to breathe at the surface of the water. Also the nostrils and the auditory openings can be tightly closed. Eyes, nostrils and ears are placed at the same level and when the crocodile is swimming just below the surface, they protrude above the water.

All crocodilians are carnivorous. Young individuals feed on insects, small fish, molluscs and crustaceans, progressing as they grow older to reptiles, fish, birds and mammals. In coping with a particularly large prey which has been drowned beforehand, they take a strong bite into it and then start rotating rapidly round their own axis tearing out pieces of meat together with bones; these they crush with their powerful teeth and then devour. Larger crocodiles can be dangerous even to human beings.

With the exception of one species, all alligators and caimans of the family Alligatoridae live in America. The largest of them is the North American Alligator *(Alligator mississippiensis);* usually 4 metres long, it can exceptionally attain a length of 6 metres. It inhabits rivers and swamps of the southern parts of the USA. For her clutch of eggs, the female gathers water plants, fallen branches and leaves, and using her snout she builds a mound at the water's edge, about 1 metre in height. She then deposits her eggs in the centre of this, covers them with soil and keeps watch over them. The Black Caiman *(Melanosuchus niger)*, related to the alligators, lives in the Amazon basin and may grow to a length of 5 metres.

The true crocodiles (family Crocodylidae) live in America, Africa, Australia, the southern and south-eastern parts of Asia, the Greater Sunda Islands and the Philippines. The most widely known species is the Nile Crocodile *(Crocodylus niloticus)* which was once distributed in vast multitudes throughout the central and southern regions of Africa. It could also be found in the estuary of the Nile, along the shores of the Mediterranean and in Palestine. It may grow to about 5 metres in length. The Giant Estuarine Crocodile *(Crocodylus porosus)*, which ranges from Ceylon and the Indian coast to the Philippines and Australia, is a notorious man-eater. It often attains a length of 6 metres. When roaming the sea, members of this species often stray far off the coast and reach the various islands of the Malay Archipelago.

The last family of the Crocodylia comprises the gavials (Gavialidae), represented today by one species only. This is the Indian Gavial *(Gavialis gangeticus)*, a very rare and strictly protected inhabitant of the Indian rivers Indus, Ganges and Brahmaputra. It can reach a length of as much as 7 metres but is not dangerous to man. It feeds on fish, frogs and water birds which it catches by its particularly long and narrow, well-toothed snout. The Gavial used to be worshipped as a sacred animal in India.

Geckos

The geckos constitute a family in the suborder Lacertilia. Their four limbs are well developed and their body is covered by small scales. The teeth are firmly rooted in the jawbones. The transparent eyelids are, as a rule, fused and immovable, and the geckos frequently lick them with their long tongues.

Geckos are capable of uttering loud sounds and, besides crocodiles and some turtles, are the only reptiles having a

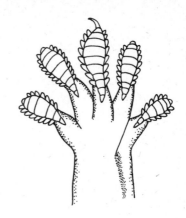

Fig. 9. Underside of a gecko's foot
(*Tarentola mauretanica*)

genuine laryngeal voice. Most geckos have digits specially adapted for walking on smooth, vertical walls, and even on glass or ceilings. The flattened tips of their digits have retractile plates on their underside; each of these bears a multitude of microscopic filaments furnished with tiny hooks that can penetrate even the most minute splits and irregularities and take fast hold. Some geckos also have clinging devices at the end of their tail or on its underside. Others, for example the European Naked-toed Kotchyi's Gecko *(Cyrtodactylus kotschyi)*, have no clinging pads at all and yet are capable of nimbly climbing along vertical walls to which they adhere with sharp little claws.

The most primitive forms of geckos have movable eyelids, whereas the large eyes of developmentally more advanced species are covered with translucent 'spectacles' that have developed from the lower eyelids. Nocturnal species have pupils which contract to a vertical split, while in diurnal species the pupil is circular.

With the exception of several viviparous species from New Zealand, gecko females lay eggs with a flexible white shell which hardens soon after laying.

The strong, tough egg shell and the geckos' habit of depositing eggs under the bark of trees have enabled some of them to enlarge considerably the range of their distribution. The eggs can survive in salt water for a number of months, and can thus be carried to great distances by ocean currents, drifting along on logs. When the surf throws the logs to a convenient shore, young geckos leave the eggs to develop and multiply far away from their original home.

Most geckos live on insects and spiders — the bigger species also include smaller vertebrates in their diet. During the evening and night hours, geckos like to gather near electric lamps located near human dwellings where insects swarm in large numbers.

In natural conditions the geckos have many enemies. The young, measuring no more than one or two centimetres, are often trapped in cobwebs; small and even adult geckos fall an easy prey to other reptiles, birds and mammals.

The largest gecko species live in the tropics and grow to a length of about 40 cm. Some species are amongst the smallest of vertebrates, measuring less than 2 cm when fully grown.

Iguanids, Agamids and Chameleons

The family of iguanids (Iguanidae) comprises lacertilians with crests on their heads and backs, strong limbs and fleshy tongues. Their range is restricted to tropical and subtropical regions of the American continent. No iguanids are found in south-eastern Europe, the mild zone of Asia or Australia, where another family, the agamids (Agamidae), have replaced them.

Iguanids and agamids usually range from 20 to 30 cm in length. The smallest of them measure only 8 — 13 cm, the largest iguanids may grow up to a length of more than 2 metres; the size of agamids very rarely exceeds 1 metre.

There is a striking similarity between some iguanids and agamids. Although the area of distribution of both families is very different, the animals of each group have developed through the centuries in much the same way under similar living conditions, that is in parallel or convergently. Thus, for instance, the thick body and prickly tail of the South American desert iguanids — the weapon-tails (genus *Hoplocercus*)

— are strongly reminiscent of the spiny-tailed agamids (genus *Uromastyx*) from the African deserts. The South American iguanids — basilisks (genus *Basiliscus*) — have their larger counterpart in the East Indian water lizards of the genus *Hydrosaurus*. These agamids are usually found on river banks. They have high crests on their backs and can rear up and run on their hind legs in an erect posture. Both iguanids and agamids have developed equally grotesque types: the former, for instance, include the Horned Toad *(Phrynosoma cornutum)*, while the Australian Moloch *(Moloch horridus)* is also a curious member of the agamid family. Both these odd reptiles, resembling small mythical dragons, live in arid regions and feed mainly on large ants.

As well as inhabiting geographically different regions, the two families also differ in certain anatomical characteristics, one of which is the position of teeth in the jaws.

Like the American iguanids, the agamids include a number of transitory forms ranging from predominantly aquatic animals to steppe and desert dwellers. The steppe species are often diggers outstandingly adapted to a partially subterranean life. Many iguanid and agamid species spend most of their life in trees. Some agamids, for example the small Indo-Malayan Flying Lizard *(Draco volans)*, can glide through the air over relatively long distances with the aid of a special parachute-like device. The hind ribs in this species are greatly elongated and interconnected with skin membranes. If the animal wants to get from one place to another, it springs off, stretches out its ribs and sails in a gliding flight from one tree to another, frequently as far as 60 metres.

Chameleons (Chamaeleonidae) are among the best-known lizards. They are separated into slightly more than 80 species, most of which come from Africa south of the Sahara and from Madagascar; only four species live elsewhere, namely in the southern parts of Europe, on the Arabian Peninsula, in India and on Ceylon.

The body of all chameleons is laterally compressed and the back is sharply ridged. The head bears projections of various shapes: some chameleons have high crests rising immediately behind the eyes and adorning the back of their head, others have movable scaly flaps on the neck. One species from Madagascar has a massive 'helmet' covering its head and its upper jaw ends in a long and pointed horn. Still other species are characterized by several such horns on their heads.

Chameleons are typical arboreal reptiles and their legs are exceptionally well adapted to moving about in branches. On each limb, two digits are opposed to the other three forming a gripping device which acts like a pair of tongs. Their prehensile tail gives them a sure hold on even the thinnest branches. The protruding eyes are covered by fused scaly eyelids in the centre of which there is a small opening for the pupil. The eyes can move independently of each other so that the animal can turn each one in different directions and observe two separate objects at a time. The chameleon's tongue serves as a perfect insect-trap: it is very long and always ready to shoot out at an amazing speed to a great distance—in some species as far as 30 cm.

A truly remarkable quality of chameleons is their ability to change colour. The change is brought about by the mechanical contraction and dilation of variously coloured pigment cells concealed in the skin. As a result, some chameleon species can change their colour rapidly and conspicuously, adapting it to that of the surroundings. The males may often change colour even when fighting against each other.

Chameleons mostly feed on insects, but larger species also hunt small vertebrates. Typical of the chameleons is the slow prowling movement by which they approach their prey. They are capable of accurately estimating its distance and only when they are quite sure that it is within their reach do they shoot out their tongue and precisely hit the insect with the tip of their tongue.

Most chameleons are oviparous. The females bury their eggs deep into the ground, and leave them, taking no further care of their offspring. There are also some viviparous species. The size of the smallest of these peculiar reptiles is only about 4 cm when fully grown, the largest species may attain a length of almost a metre.

Lizards and Skinks

The representatives of the family of typical lizards (Lacertidae) are found in the Old World: in Europe, Asia, Africa and in a part of the Indo-Australian region. All of them have a slender, cylindrical body, well-developed legs and a long, slender tail.

Lizards are small or medium-sized reptiles. The Ocellated Lizard *(Lacerta lepida)* is the only one to attain the exceptional length of 80 cm. The majority of lacertids, however, never grow to be more than 20—30 cm. There may be conspicuous differences in the coloration of males and females belonging to the same species: in the European Sand Lizard *(Lacerta agilis)*, for example, the females are brownish and the males greenish. In other cases, the animal may change its coloration in the course of its life: when young, the Balkan Green Lizard *(Lacerta trilineata)* from the Balkans is brown with whitish-yellow longitudinal streaks running along its back, but when it reaches the adult stage this colour is replaced by bright green. Also the animals' behaviour is closely related to the differences in coloration. When in danger, the dark-coloured young always hide on the ground, under leaves, among twigs and stones or under shrubs, whereas adult lizards seek safety in the tops of bushes or trees, among green leaves or in grass.

All lizards lay eggs, the only exception being the Viviparous Lizard *(Lacerta vivipara)* that gives birth to fully developed young. Even here, however, it is a case of pseudoviviparity (ovoviviparity) and depends on the climate: in the north and in the cool mountain climate this lizard bears its young directly, while in the southern parts of its range, where the climate permits the development of eggs outside the mother's body, it occasionally becomes an egg-layer. Clutches of eggs are deposited by the female under stones, among leaves, and in similar places. The lizard spends the cold winter season in a wide variety of shelters.

Lizards present various interesting adaptations to their habitat and ways of life: the tail of arboreal species, for example, bears a ring of pointed or hook-like scales which help them in climbing. Due to their coloration, the desert lacertids of the genus *Eremias,* which inhabit the arid regions of Africa and the semi-deserts of south-western and central Asia, completely merge with their environment. Their back is sand-coloured and adorned with a series of circular light spots resembling small pebbles. The fringe-toed lacertids of the genus *Acanthodactylus* are the best adapted to life in deserts. The feet of some species bear projecting scales which act rather like snowshoes. These species are also expert burrowers.

Lizards, like many other lacertilians, have a remarkable faculty of passive defence: their caudal vertebrae contain small plates of thinned bone tissue where the tail can easily break off. The shed tail distracts the enemy's attention and enables the lizard to escape. It takes a short time for the new tail to regenerate, the only difference being that, instead of containing true bony vertebrae, the new portion is supported by a solid ligament.

Another family to be mentioned here are the skinks (Scincidae) that are found in America, the Indo-Australian region, Africa, Madagascar, southern Asia and southern Europe. They all have a long, cylindrical body and short limbs which may be rudimentary in some species, or even completely missing. Their body is covered with shiny, smooth scales.

Skinks live hidden under leaves or stones, many of them even underground. In the subterranean species the eyes are protected by special eyelids, and both nostrils and auditory orifices can be tightly closed. It is also in these forms that limbs remain underdeveloped.

Most skinks are carnivorous, feeding mainly on insects. Some species, however, are herbivorous. In contrast to the former, the herbivorous skinks have blunt teeth adapted to grinding plant food.

Some skinks lay eggs, others are viviparous. While the females of oviparous species lay clutches frequently containing more than 20 eggs, the viviparous species usually bear smaller broods of two to ten young. The smaller species measure only about 5 cm, whilst the largest can reach a length of 75 cm. One of the largest is the Blue-tongued Skink *(Tiliqua scin-*

coides) of Australia, a species which shows a curious defensive behaviour: when in danger, it opens its mouth wide and thrusts out its exceptionally long, bluish-purple tongue, waving it to and fro.

Monitor Lizards and Gila Monsters

The monitor lizards (Varanidae) are the most advanced lacertilians. Their elongate body with a long, thick tail is carried by well-developed, strong legs furnished with powerful claws. The elongate head is carried on a long neck, the forked tongue can be flicked out to a great distance, and the teeth are sharp and curved backwards.

These lizards may be terrestrial, arboreal or burrowing animals; some of them live in close proximity to rivers and lakes. Their home is Africa, all the warm regions of Asia, the Indo-Australian region and Australia.

The biggest lizard in the world is the Komodo Dragon *(Varanus komodoensis)* which can reach a length of about 3 metres and a weight of approximately 130 kg. Its distribution is restricted to the Lesser Sunda Islands of Komodo, Flores, and the islets Rintja and Padar. It was not discovered and described until 1912, although numerous tales had long been told among the natives about dragons from the island of Komodo from whose mouths flames leapt and which were said to be dangerous to man. The very long tongue of this animal is bright yellowish-orange in colour, and when the animal flickers it out little imagination is needed to see it as a flashing flame. After 1912 the islands became the destination of numerous scientific and hunting expeditions which caused the Komodo Dragon to be brought almost to extinction. The landing of ships on the island is now prohibited and scientific observations and capture of the species are allowed in exceptional cases only.

The Komodo Dragon feeds mostly on wild pigs, small deer and other larger mammals. Young individuals eat birds' eggs and hunt small prey. Besides strong jaws equipped with sharp teeth, its powerful tail is a formidable weapon with which it can cause serious wounds, even to man.

The family Helodermatidae is represented by two isolated North American species—the Beaded Lizard *(Heloderma horridum)*, which attains a length of 80 cm, and the somewhat smaller Gila Monster *(Heloderma suspectum)*. These are the only lacertilians to have developed venom glands and grooved fangs. Grooved teeth are located in both jaws, while the venom glands—in contrast to those of venomous snakes—are found only in the lower jaw.

The Gila Monster has a stout body, a powerful tail, and legs equipped with strong claws. The scales covering the body are arranged so that they abut one another like horny corals: they do not overlap, as in other reptiles.

Gila Monsters are carnivorous, feeding on other animals' eggs, as well as on the young of mammals and birds. They hunt after nightfall, guided by their sense of smell. When following a trail, they touch the ground with their long tongue at short intervals and convey information picked up on its tip to a specialised organ of smell located on the palate.

Legless Lizards

Besides animals with normally developed limbs, the Lacertilia also includes species with either one or both pairs of legs incompletely developed. Thus they have lost the characteristic lizard-like appearance, and superficially resemble snakes or even worms.

The worm lizards (Amphisbaenidae) have long, worm-like bodies which, from above, appear to be segmented. A very few species have developed minute fore limbs but, for the most part, they have no legs at all. They spend most of their life underground. Curiously, when placed on the ground, they move in a straight line. Their diet consists of earthworms, termites, ants, and their larvae and pupae. Only the left lung is developed. Amphisbaenids usually reach a length of about 30 cm, but some species may exceed 75 cm (for example the

African genus *Monopeltis*). They range throughout the tropical zone of America, Africa and south-eastern Asia. The only European species is *Blanus cinereus*, which is found in Spain.

Another family of legless lizards, the Anguidae, includes the common European Slow-worm *(Anguis fragilis)* and its large south European relative, the European Glass Lizard *(Ophisaurus apodus)*. A more detailed account of both these species is given in the illustrated section of this book.

Australia, Tasmania and New Guinea are the home of slender snake-like lizards without fore legs which belong to the family of flap-footed lizards (Pygopodidae). Their hind legs are reduced to small flaps, about 1 cm long, situated close to the anus. These animals grow to a length of 70 cm and, like slow-worms in their body shape and way of life, anatomically they are closely allied to the geckos.

Four species of small and slender legless lizards, about 30 cm long, come from equatorial Africa. These are members of the genus *Feylinia* which live in decayed logs and in the nests of termites on which they feed almost exclusively.

Boas and Pythons

The other suborder in the Squamata — the snakes (Ophidia) — is most abundantly represented in tropical and subtropical regions. However, some snakes are known to occur in the far North, even beyond the Polar Circle, and others can be found as far south as Patagonia in South America.

One of the characteristics common to all the snakes is the absence of limbs. It is only certain primitive groups that have preserved vestiges of the pelvis, or even minute remnants of hind limbs, on their skeleton. The snake skull reveals some peculiarities, notably the flexible, extendable ligaments connecting the jaws and enabling most snakes to swallow their prey whole, even if it is relatively large. This is also why the teeth of snakes are not adapted to chewing but only to grasping the prey and pushing it into the gullet. The teeth are acicular, sharp and frequently curved backwards. In venomous

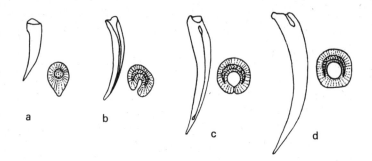

Fig. 10. Types of snake teeth:
a) smooth tooth, b) grooved tooth, c) grooved hollow tooth, d) hollow tooth

snakes, certain teeth in the upper jaw are considerably enlarged and either hollow or grooved; they are connected with the outlet of the venom gland. By muscular pressure the venom is ejected into the wound either through the tooth or along the groove.

The tongue of snakes is an organ of touch, smell and taste. It is narrow, forked and highly extendable. The lungs are characteristic and related to the shape of their body: only the right pulmonary lobe is developed, the left is either entirely absent or underdeveloped.

Snakes devour their prey — mostly vertebrates — in one piece. They have several ways of killing it: some of them do so by constricting it in the loops of their body and suffocating it, others by pressing it to the ground, still others by striking it. Many snakes devour their prey alive.

The locomotory organs of snakes are the amazingly numerous ribs, which vary in number between about 180 and 445 depending on the species. They are joined by means of a muscular layer to the ventral plates which serve as a support against the irregularities of the ground. The movement of ribs thus causes the typical undulations of the moving snake.

The giant constricting snakes (Boidae) include true boas and pythons. The family is an ancient one and its members have vestiges of the pelvis and hind limbs on the skeleton. True boas usually give birth to fully developed young, while pythons are oviparous. The mother snake coils herself around her clutch of leathery eggs, warming them with the heat of her own body which, at that time, exceeds the temperature of the surrounding environment by several degrees.

Members of the Boidae live in tropical and subtropical regions, their range being discontinuous. They are, as a rule, very powerful snakes. The Reticulate Python *(Python reticulatus)* from south-eastern Asia attains a length of slightly over 9 metres and a weight of more than 100 kg. The largest of the true boas, the South-American Giant Anaconda *(Eunectes murinus)*, is still more robust: although it equals the former species in length, it weighs more than 150 kg. The Boa Constrictor *(Constrictor constrictor)* and the Cuban Boa *(Epicrates angulifer)* may grow to a length of 5 metres. The only European representative of boas, the Sand Boa *(Eryx jaculus)*, is a relative dwarf—only rarely does it attain 80 cm in length. Even so, it is a typical boa in both body shape and behaviour and, just like its larger relatives, it suffocates its prey—usually small rodents and lizards—by coiling around it.

Burrowing Snakes

The relatively numerous small members of the family of blind burrowing snakes (Typhlopidae) are the opposite of huge pythons and boas. At first sight they do not look like snakes at all, reminding us more of large earthworms in their coloration and body shape. Closer investigation, however, will reveal two little black spots, which are the eyes, at one end of their body. The internal anatomy of these small snakes clearly shows them to be typical vertebrates with a characteristic skeleton and other organs. All typhlopids have larger or smaller skeletal vestiges of limbs. The largest species are about 75 cm long. Some of them are oviparous and others are viviparous.

All these small subterranean snakes live in warm regions

and one species is found even in Europe—the Worm Snake *(Typhlops vermicularis)* which is about 30 cm long. Its still smaller relative from south-eastern Asia, the Flower-pot Snake *(Typhlops braminus)*, has become cosmopolitan thanks to man: with cultivated plants in flowerpots, it has been transported to all parts of the world. It has been found in Mexico, on the Hawaian Islands, on Madagascar, and also on a great number of islands in the Pacific.

Non-venomous and Venomous Colubrids

Representatives of the large family of colubrid snakes (Colubridae) can be found all over the world. This family comprises both non-venomous species with smooth teeth and venomous species with grooved teeth. In the latter group, the fangs are located in the rear of the jaws under the eyes, and not in the front part of the mouth as in the case of vipers and rattle-snakes.

The largest groups are the subfamilies Natricinae and Colubrinae, many of which occur in Europe. They include small snakes not exceeding 50 cm in length, as well as snakes which—besides boas and pythons—are among the longest snakes of the world. The biggest European colubrid is the Large Whip Snake *(Coluber jugularis)* which can reach a length of up to 3 metres; Asian species of the genus *Zaocys* often grow almost a metre longer than this.

The American king snakes (genus *Lampropeltis*) may doubtless be regarded as the most beautiful colubers. The body of some of them is ringed with alternating white, red and black bands or is flecked all over with coloured spots. In pattern and coloration, some species resemble the extremely venomous North American coral snakes. Some of the European colubrids are beautifully coloured, one of the most notable being *Elaphe situla* of the chicken-snake group.

Due to ignorance, people often believe the harmless colubrids to be dangerous snakes and unnecessarily exterminate them. In some countries, however, these snakes are kept almost as domestic animals and are even intentionally brought to human habitations. Such a favoured species is the Cape File Snake *(Mehelya capensis)*, more than 2 m long, from the eastern parts of South Africa: it is exclusively a snake-eater.

Egg-eating snakes (subfamily Dasypeltinae) represent a distinct group of non-venomous colubers. They occur mostly in Africa but one species lives in southern India. Egg-eaters have scarcely any teeth but the jaws and anterior gullet are enormously distensible. A sticky mucous membrane covering the inside of the mouth prevents the egg from slipping out while being gulped down. After entering the gullet, the egg is cut open by projections on twelve specially adapted vertebrae. Behind these, there are others that crush the broken egg-shell and squeeze out the liquid contents. The snake then regurgitates the hard remnant of the egg-shell. Adult egg-eaters measure about 80 cm and are capable of devouring a mouthful as large as a hen's egg.

Venomous colubrids have well developed venom glands and longitudinally grooved venom-conducting fangs. These features also characterize the subfamily Boiginae. The African, Asian and Australian representatives of this subfamily are large venomous snakes whose food consists of small and medium-sized mammals, birds, lizards and snakes. The bite of some species, such as the Mangrove Snake *(Boiga dendrophila)* from the Indo-Malayan region and the Sunda Islands, may be fatal even to humans.

The original home of these snakes was south-western Asia and northern Africa; in past geological periods, they came over to Europe along three routes—across the Bosphorus to the Balkan Peninsula, through Gibraltar to Spain, and from Tunisia to Sicily and then Italy.

Venomous colubrids also include whip-snakes—slender, long snakes which live mostly on trees. The Painted Bronzeback *(Ahaetula nasuta)* lives in south-eastern Asia. Its extraordinarily slender body is perfectly camouflaged among the green leaves in which it lies in wait for small agamas and birds.

Elapids

The family of elapids (Elapidae) includes snakes with immovable, short and narrow venom-conducting fangs. Each fang has a groove on its anterior face, in addition to an inner duct through which the venom is conveyed. Most of the representatives of this family, particularly the large-sized species, are extremely poisonous and often fatal to man. The initial effect of their venom is a paralysis of the nervous system. They are distributed throughout the warm regions of Australia, Africa, Asia and America.

Many representatives of this family, particularly some coral snakes (genus *Micrurus*), are beautifully coloured. Cobras are remarkable for their ability to extend their cervical ribs and raise the anterior part of their body when irritated. Most elapids are egg-layers; some of them, however, give birth to fully developed young.

The largest venomous snake in the world is the King Cobra *(Ophiophagus hannah)* which, in exceptional cases, can reach a length of 6 metres. It occurs throughout East India, southeastern Asia, Indonesia and the Philippines. Its venom glands contain a large quantity of extremely strong venom. In the mating period, this cobra builds two-storied nests of sticks and leaves. Eggs are placed in the lower compartment and the female lies coiled up in the upper. The material needed for building the nest is brought by the female in a coil formed by the front part of her body. The King Cobra well deserves its Latin name which, translated into English, means 'snake-eater': it feeds mostly on snakes and lizards, although it will occasionally take small mammals.

The Indian Cobra *(Naja naja)* is 2 metres long and has a typical spectacle-shaped pattern on its expanded neck, hence its popular name—Spectacle Snake. Fakirs presenting shows with cobras are well known, but of course, in most cases, these snakes have been deprived of their fangs and are therefore far from dangerous. The music produced by the snake charmers during these shows is entirely superfluous and impresses only the spectators, as the snakes are quite deaf and their movements, suggestive of a dance, are in fact merely reactions to the movements of the snake charmer.

The Egyptian Asp *(Naja haje)* was regarded as sacred in Ancient Egypt. In all probability, it was this species which caused the death of Queen Cleopatra. The so-called Ringhals or Spitting Cobra *(Naja nigricollis)* is also well known. This species has developed the capacity to spit its finely dispersed venom from openings on the fangs to a distance of as much as 4 metres directly into the eyes of the victim, causing temporary or permanent blindness.

Closely allied to the cobras are the mambas, agile African snakes of genus *Dendroaspis*. The longest among them is the Black Mamba *(Dendroaspis polylepis)* which can grow to a length of 4.5 metres. As in related species, its venom is extremely effective.

Coral snakes (genus *Micrurus*) comprise another venomous group. The most notorious of these, the North American Coral Snake *(Micrurus fulvius)*, is distributed from Mexico to the southern parts of the USA. Although it is not a large snake (only exceptionally does it attain a length of 2 metres), its venom is very strong indeed. Fortunately it is not aggressive.

Australia is the home of more than 80 snake species of the family Elapidae, many of which are extremely dangerous. One of them, the Taipan *(Oxyuranus scutellatus)*, exceeds 3 metres in length and has perhaps the most powerful venom of all snakes. A man bitten by the Taipan usually dies within a few minutes. Another Australian snake, outwardly resembling the vipers, is the Death Adder *(Acanthophis antarcticus)*. The snakes of the Australian genera *Pseudechis* and *Notechis* are also deadly. Some of them attack the victim so violently that the assault resembles a swift leap.

Sea Snakes

In the animal kingdom, there are many examples of originally terrestrial animals becoming secondarily adapted to life in the sea. Within the Ophidia, this lifestyle is shown by the venomous sea snakes (Hydrophidae) of which there are about 50 species.

These snakes, which are often more than 3 metres long, are adjusted exclusively to marine life and are excellent swimmers. In the Indian Ocean and in the Pacific, large 'shoals' of sea snakes can be observed swimming close to the surface usually in the early morning or late afternoon. All species live in open tropical and subtropical seas, only exceptionally are some of them found in fresh water. They form an outstanding ecological group whose body shape is perfectly adapted to aquatic life. Their tail is usually laterally flattened and the nostrils, which lie in the upper part of the snout, are provided with special valves. They usually have a small head and a very slender and long neck; the rest of the body is much bulkier. This specialized shape is associated with their aquatic existence and with their method of hunting: the massive abdominal portion anchors the body in water while the long and thin anterior part thrusts itself at the prey. Smaller fish, especially eels, are their main food. Their venom is very potent but as these snakes are not aggressive, cases of attacks on man are extremely rare.

Sea snakes are mostly viviparous and the young are born in water. A few species of the genus *Laticauda* come ashore to lay eggs. Only these are capable of moving about on land, whereas all the other sea snakes are completely powerless out of water. If they are washed ashore beyond the tidemark by the waves, they cannot survive and soon die.

Sea snakes of the subfamily Laticaudinae inhabit the seas adjacent to the Bay of Bengal, off Japan, Australia and the Pacific islands. Japanese fishermen catch them in great quantities because of their palatable meat.

Vipers and Rattlesnakes

Vipers and rattlesnakes are among the most advanced venomous snakes. Their long, powerful fangs are hollow and function as hypodermic needles. When at rest, these fangs are folded backwards in the mouth cavity and become erect only with the opening of the snake's mouth. The venom glands are relatively big and their venom is extremely powerful.

The true vipers (family Viperidae) are confined to the Old World (Europe, Asia and Africa). They are most abundant in warm regions, and in the mild zone they gradually become less frequent. In colder regions, for example in northern Europe, only specially adapted species are known to exist. The Adder *(Vipera berus)* is the only one to be found in the far North, where it extends just beyond the Arctic Circle.

Russell's Viper *(Vipera russelli)*, which occurs from India and Ceylon to the Malay Peninsula, Java and Sumatra, is beautifully coloured. It is one of the snakes whose venom is dangerous but it is not aggressive. It may grow to a length of almost 2 metres. A much-feared snake of North and East Africa, India, Ceylon and central Asia is the Saw-scaled Viper *(Echis carinatus)*, a small species which reaches a length of no more than 70 cm. A great many people fall a victim to it every year.

North Africa is the home of the Horned Viper *(Cerastes cerastes)*. This small snake lives in inhospitable sand and stone deserts where it buries itself up to its eyes in fine sand, especially in dried up river-beds.

The largest vipers belong to the African genus *Bitis*. A true giant is the Gaboon Viper *(Bitis gabonica)* from equatorial Africa, which reaches 2 metres in length. It is very stout and heavy and its fangs may be as long as 5 cm, yet it uses them only in hunting prey; it never attacks man, even in a state of extreme agitation, and deters the enemy only by a loud hissing and by swelling its body. Like the other vipers, it uses its movable fangs not only in striking its prey but also in pushing it from the mouth into the gullet.

On the American continent, the family of pit-vipers (Crotalidae) takes the place of vipers. Its representatives are also found in southern and south-eastern Asia. Only one species of this type, the Siberian Tiger Snake *(Agkistrodon halys)*, is found in eastern Europe.

The pit-vipers have a special circular sense organ behind the nostrils which is lacking in vipers. It is formed by a small hollow, the bottom of which is covered by a fine membrane, thickly interwoven with projections of nerve cells. For a long time, this organ was considered to be an organ of smell, or of hearing, or even a secretory organ. As late as in 1937, it was discovered that this peculiar organ, unique in the animal kingdom (it exists in another form only in the Boidae), perceives warm-blooded animals by their body heat. It is so sensitive, that, at a short distance, it can even distinguish an animal whose body temperature exceeds the temperature of the surrounding air by only 0.5° C. This organ enables the pit-vipers to follow and hunt their prey by night. Since the majority of these snakes are nocturnal, the heat-sensitive hollow helps them to locate a bird's nest or a rodent's den containing the young.

The best known pit-vipers are those in which the end of the tail is modified into a rattle composed of a series of segments, formed by the fusion of horny skin and tail bones; these seg-

Fig. 11. A rattlesnake's rattle

ments are loosely attached to each other so that a rapid vibration of the tail produces the typical rattling sound that acts as a warning to discourage bigger animals from approaching the snake. The species with a rattle are evolutionarily more advanced than those in which it is absent. The largest pit-viper with no rattle is the Bushmaster *(Lachesis muta)* inhabiting the virgin rain forests of Central and South America. It often grows to a length of slightly over 3 metres and is relatively rare. The largest of the true rattlesnakes is the Eastern Diamondback *(Crotalus adamanteus)* from the south-eastern regions of the USA, its maximum length being nearly 3 metres.

Olm

(Cave Salamander)
Proteus anguinus

A cave-dwelling aquatic amphibian with an an-guilliform, elongate, non-pigmented body and a long dorso-ventrally flattened head The tail is laterally flattened and is provided with a fin edge both above and beneath. Limbs are short, with three digits on each fore limb and two on each hind leg. The skin covering the eyes of adult animals renders them functionless; in the young the eyes are visible as tiny red dots. Bright red external gills are situated behind the head.

It is found in the karst region of north-western Yugoslavia, in cool, clean and sluggish subterra-nean waters. When foraging for food, which con-sists mainly of water-fleas and various worms, it is directed by smell. Olms inhabiting cool under-ground waters are, as a rule, viviparous. If, how-ever, the temperature of water exceeds 15° C, the females lay single eggs that hatch after approxi-mately three months; the young are about 2 cm long and closely resemble the adults.

It can be kept in a shaded glass aquarium con-taining no vegetation. The depth of water should not be more than ·40 cm, and the temperature 8—14° C.

LENGTH:
25—30 cm.
BREEDING SEASON:
Throughout the year; does not undergo metamorphosis; breeds whilst still in the larval form (neoteny).

1 — adult
2 — young

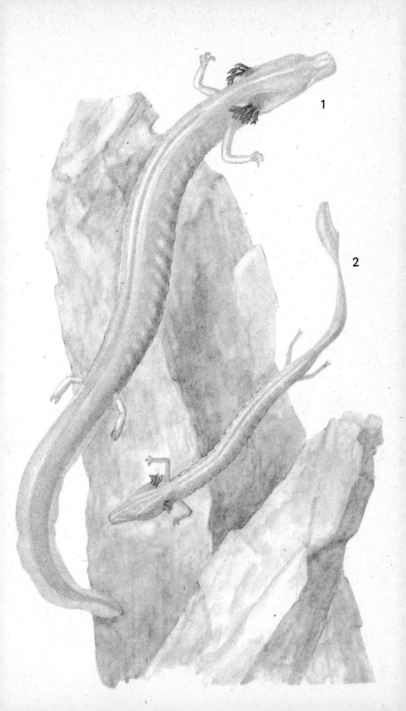

Fire Salamander

(European Salamander)
Salamandra salamandra

It has a glossy black body with marked ribbing and irregularly scattered spots ranging in colour from yolk-yellow to orange; in west European specimens, these spots can fuse into longitudinal streaks. The skin is smooth; on either side of the rear part of the head there are two crescent-shaped dermal glands which contain a venomous secretion. Body and head are dorso-ventrally flattened; the blunt tail is circular in cross-section.

It ranges throughout the hills and mountains of southern and central Europe, eastern Asia and north-western Africa, where it lives in damp, deciduous woods to altitudes of more than 1,000 metres, in the vicinity of clean and cool streams. Throughout the day it stays under stones, bark or leaves, coming out of hiding only in the evening, at night or in rainy weather. It feeds on various invertebrates — worms, slugs and insects — and hibernates in underground shelters which it leaves in March or April. The mating period starts shortly afterwards. The female enters water to bear 50 or more larvae with four fully developed limbs and branchial gills. There are several subspecies.

It can be kept in a cool aquaterrarium at a temperature of 12—18° C.

LENGTH:
20—28 cm.
BREEDING SEASON:
March and April; eggs are often fertilized in the following year; the larvae hatch in spring and metamorphose after 2—3 months.

1 — eastern form
2 — western form
3 — larvae

1

2

3

Alpine Salamander
Salamandra atra

Salamandridae

Golden-striped Salamander
Chioglossa lusitanica

The Alpine Salamander is a uniform glossy black with marked cross-ribs on the sides. The flanks bear a row of large warts. Large crescent-shaped venom glands are situated behind the head.

It occurs in the Alps, in the French Jura and in mountains of western Yugoslavia and Albania, where it lives in shady woods rich in clean streams. Like the Fire Salamander, it is active in the evening and by night. The composition of food and the mating period are also the same. However, the Alpine Salamander does not pass through any free living larval stage: after one year's pregnancy, the female gives birth to two completely developed young.

The Golden-striped Salamander, distinguished by two metallic, copper-coloured longitudinal streaks running along its back and by an extremely long tail, is distributed throughout Spain and Portugal, in mountains overgrown with deciduous forests. It lives near springs and rocky streams, hiding under rocks and logs in the daytime and active in the dark when it hunts various insects using its long tongue. It is very agile and can shed its tail when in danger. Fertilized eggs are laid by the female in swiftly flowing currents. The larvae are long and thin, with short legs and a very long tail which has a broad, fin-shaped edging.

Both these salamanders may be kept in a well-covered, cool aquaterrarium with high aerial humidity and plenty of hiding places.

Salamandra atra:
LENGTH:
13—16 cm.
BREEDING SEASON:
March and April; fully developed young are born in spring of the following year.

Chioglossa lusitanica:
LENGTH:
12—15 cm.
BREEDING SEASON:
Spring.

1 — *Salamandra atra*
2 — *Chioglossa lusitanica*

1

2

Sharp-ribbed Salamander

Salamandridae

(Spanish Ribbed Newt)
Pleurodeles waltl

Sardinian Brook Salamander

(Sardinian Newt or Flat-headed Salamander)
Euproctus platycephalus

The Sharp-ribbed Salamander is one of the biggest European salamanders. The colour of its young ranges from dirty yellow to olive green and the adults are greyish-brown. Their body is decorated with dark irregular spots on a lighter background. The large and pointed warts on both sides of the body are yellowish-white to orange. The tail in males is provided with an orange fin.

It inhabits the Iberian Peninsula and north-western Morocco and prefers places near water. It spends the day hidden under stones or in moss and becomes active only after dark. Its diet consists of various invertebrates as well as small tadpoles and newts. It produces loud, quacking sounds, especially when in danger. The female attaches her eggs to water plants, drifting pieces of wood, or stones.

The Sardinian Brook Salamander, distinguished by its grainy skin, lives in the vicinity of mountain streams in Sardinia. It feeds on various invertebrates and often hibernates in deep burrows. Its eggs are attached to stones submerged in water currents.

Both these amphibians may be kept in a cool aquaterrarium.

Pleurodeles waltl:
LENGTH:
25—30 cm.
BREEDING SEASON:
Usually all the year round; frequently neotenic.

Euproctus platycephalus:
LENGTH:
15—18 cm.
BREEDING SEASON:
May to July, depending on the latitude; the larvae metamorphose the following spring.

1 — *Pleurodeles waltl*
2 — *Euproctus platycephalus*

Alpine Newt
Triturus alpestris

The back of the male Alpine Newt is dark-coloured, the sides are bluish, the belly orange-red and in the breeding season a crest of skin develops on the back. Females have no crest and are less colourful.

It lives in central and southern Europe near mountain lakes, pools and brooks, to an altitude of 3,000 metres. Its diet is made up of various aquatic and terrestrial invertebrates. It hibernates on land, takes to the water very early in spring — in southern Europe often as early as February, in more northerly regions later on — and mates immediately. The larvae are 7—8 mm long on hatching and metamorphose after reaching the length of about 3—4 cm, usually in August and September; sometimes they hibernate in water (in cool spring waters, fountains, etc.) and their development is completed the following summer. Several subspecies occur in Europe.

It may be kept in a cool aquaterrarium or in an aquarium provided with floating plants and pieces of bark.

LENGTH:
8—12 cm.
BREEDING SEASON:
March to May;
larvae
metamorphose in
August and
September.

1 — female
(above)
2-3 — male (left,
below)
4-5 — larvae of
various ages

Crested Newt
(Great Warty Newt)
Triturus cristatus

Salamandridae

A solidly built newt with a dark, occasionally black-spotted back and an orange belly with large dark spots. The skin is covered with wart-like growths. In the breeding season, the male has a strong spiky crest on its back which is interrupted at the base of the tail but continues along its top and bottom edges. Females have only a narrow edging on the tail.

It occurs from southern and central Europe to western Asia, living in or near stagnant waters or slow, sluggish streams overgrown with water plants. Arthropods, worms and small newts form the adult diet, whereas the larvae feed on plankton crustaceans, aquatic insects and other invertebrates. It hibernates on land in fallen leaves, under stones or pieces of wood. Early in spring it returns to the water to mate. The female attaches her 200—400 eggs, one by one, to water plants and submerged stones. The development of larvae lasts about three months; they are light-coloured and have a thin elongated end to the tail. There are several subspecies.

It can be kept either in a cool aquaterrarium or in an aquarium provided with aquatic plants and floating twigs and bark.

LENGTH:
16—18 cm.
BREEDING SEASON:
March and April;
larvae
metamorphose in
June.

1 — female
2 — male

Smooth Newt
(Common Newt)
Triturus vulgaris

Salamandridae

The basic colour of the body is olive-brown, speckled in males with circular black spots. In the breeding period, males are adorned with a high, unbroken crest starting immediately behind the head and terminating at the end of the tail where it is developed on both dorsal and ventral edges. In the smaller females the crest is absent and the colour varies from brownish to yellowish-brown.

The Smooth Newt is distributed throughout Europe, ranging from the British Isles to central Siberia, northwards as far as southern Scandinavia; it avoids, however, regions covered with continuous forests. It can be found even in the smallest pools and lives on a large variety of invertebrates. As early as the end of February it leaves its winter shelters and pairs in water. The female attaches the 200—300 eggs to water plants; the aquatic larvae complete their development in about three months, though they may take somewhat longer in colder waters. Soon after mating the adult newts leave the water to live in damp places nearby. Under natural conditions, the Smooth Newt sometimes successfully interbreeds with the Carpathian Newt *(Triturus montandoni).* There are many subspecies in southern Europe.

It can be kept in a cold aquaterrarium offering plenty of natural shelters.

LENGTH:
8—10 cm.
BREEDING SEASON:
April and May;
larvae
metamorphose in
June and July.

1 — male —
aquatic stage
2 — female —
aquatic stage
3 — larva
4 — terrestrial
stage

Carpathian Newt

(Montandon's Newt)

Triturus montandoni

Salamandridae

The back and sides of the body are olive-green to brownish, darkly spotted in the male. The belly is orange-red. The skin is rough and granulated. No crest is developed along the back of either sex, but a low ridge runs along the middle of the dorsal surface and passes into the upper edging of the tail. In males, the tail gradually tapers off into a thin extension that may attain 8 mm in length.

This species occurs in the Carpathian mountains where it lives in forests close to stagnant or slowly flowing waters, ranging in altitude from 500 to 2,000 metres above sea level. When in water, it feeds mainly on insect larvae, frogs' spawn and aquatic molluscs; when on dry land, it eats insects and worms. It appears in water soon after the snow has melted and pairs soon afterwards. The larvae hatch 2—3 weeks after the eggs are laid. Their metamorphosis usually takes place in summer, but in cold waters they sometimes hibernate in the larval stage. Adult newts leave the water soon after mating and live in woods under moss, leaves, branches and stones.

The Carpathian Newt can be kept in a cold aquaterrarium.

LENGTH:
7—10 cm.
BREEDING SEASON:
April and May;
the larvae
metamorphose in
July and August.

1 — male
2 — female
3 — larva

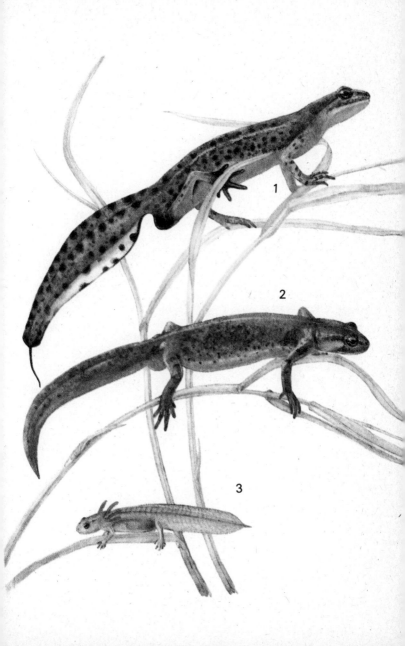

Marbled Newt
Triturus marmoratus

Salamandridae

Sardinian Cave Salamander
(Brown Cave Salamander)
Hydromantes genei

Plethodontidae

The Marbled Newt is considered one of the most beautiful European newts. It has a conspicuous brick-red dorsal edging running along the green, black-marbled back and tail. It occurs in Portugal, Spain and western France where it lives in lowlands and hilly regions, near stagnant waters — even the smallest pools. The adults live under stones and in other damp places, feeding on various invertebrates. They leave their winter shelters as early as February and March, and, after mating in water, the females attach their eggs to water plants.

The Sardinian Cave Salamander is found in south-eastern France, Italy and Sardinia. It lives in caves and rock fissures, under stones and among fallen leaves. Being an exclusively nocturnal animal, it only leaves its shelter during the daytime in cold and wet weather. It feeds on small insects and worms, catching the prey with its long, extensible tongue. The Sardinian Cave Salamander develops without a larval stage; the female gives birth to her young on dry land. Having undeveloped lungs, this salamander breathes through the entire surface of its body.

Both these species can be kept in a cool aquaterrarium with a higher level of aerial humidity; the Sardinian Cave Salamander cannot tolerate the sun.

Triturus marmoratus:
LENGTH:
14 — 16 cm.
BREEDING SEASON:
April and May;
the larvae metamorphose in July and August.

Hydromantes genei:
LENGTH:
10 — 13 cm.
BREEDING SEASON:
February and March;
the fully developed young are born in summer.

1 — *Triturus marmoratus*
2 — *Hydromantes genei*

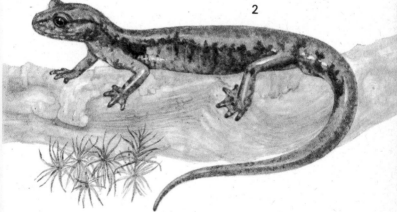

1

2

Fire-bellied Toad
Bombina bombina

Discoglossidae

Yellow-bellied Toad
(Variegated Fire Toad or Mountain Toad)
Bombina variegata

The dorsal side of the Fire-bellied Toad is greyish-black or greyish-brown with dark spots. The black belly is marked with red or orange speckles.

It lives in central and eastern Europe and is abundant in lowlands, inhabiting both small pools and larger ponds. It is an excellent swimmer. Larvae of gnats and midges, aquatic crustaceans and molluscs constitute its diet. When in danger it sometimes assumes a warning position: it turns on its back, arches its body and exposes its brightly coloured belly towards the enemy. Its skin secretions are venomous.

The back of the Yellow-bellied Toad is grey to dark-brown, frequently dark-speckled. The yellow belly is adorned with black or bluish spots.

It is widespread in southern and eastern Europe, except in the Iberian Peninsula, mostly in mountains where it reaches the elevation of 1,800 metres. Its biology is similar to that of the Fire-bellied Toad. A number of subspecies occur in Europe.

These toads thrive in an aquaterrarium at room temperature. Because of their venomous secretions, it is inadvisable to keep them with other animals.

Bombina bombina:
LENGTH:
4.5 cm.
BREEDING SEASON:
Throughout April and May; tadpoles metamorphose in September and October.

Bombina variegata:
LENGTH:
5 cm.
BREEDING SEASON:
March to May; tadpoles metamorphose in September.

1 — *Bombina bombina* — dorsal side
2 — *Bombina bombina* — ventral side
3 — *Bombina variegata*

Midwife Toad
Alytes obstetricans

Painted Frog
Discoglossus pictus

The Midwife Toad is an inconspicuous, small grey species with a warty skin and occurs in the western parts of central and southern Europe. It inhabits hilly regions near pools, ditches and other small bodies of water where it burrows in the soil or finds shelter under wood or stones. It is nocturnal and feeds on small invertebrates. It mates on land. The male winds strings of fertilized eggs around his hind legs and carries them with him all the time. When the tadpoles are about to hatch, he goes into the water where they emerge and eventually hibernate. They metamorphose in the following year.

The Painted Frog has a red, yellow or brown back with dark markings and a whitish, sometimes densely spotted underside. Its range extends from south-eastern Europe to north-western Africa where it inhabits damp meadows near rivers and brooks, swamps and peat-bogs. Like the Midwife Toad it feeds on insects, worms, slugs and other invertebrates. It is extremely fertile: one female lays several thousands of eggs every year.

Both these small frogs can be kept in a vivarium provided with a container of water, or in an aquaterrarium, at room temperature.

Alytes obstetricans:
LENGTH:
4—5 cm.
BREEDING SEASON:
April to June; tadpoles metamorphose in the following spring.

Discoglossus pictus:
LENGTH:
6—7 cm.
BREEDING SEASON:
Throughout spring and summer; tadpoles metamorphose after 1—2 months.

1-2 — *Alytes obstetricans*
3 — *Discoglossus pictus*

Common Spadefoot

(Garlic Toad)

Pelobates fuscus

Pelobatidae

This frog has a smooth skin and a light brown or grey back adorned with red dots and spots varying from olive-green to chestnut-brown. The belly is greyish-white, sometimes marked with dark speckles. The bulging eyes have a vertically contracting pupil. The inner side of each hind leg bears a conspicuous horny projection which the animal uses to bury itself rapidly in the ground.

It ranges from central Europe to western Asia and lives in lowland sandy regions. During the day it lies hidden in its underground shelter but comes out after nightfall to hunt for worms, molluscs and other invertebrates. In the breeding season it makes for water where the female winds a long string of several thousand eggs around water plants. Tadpoles hatch several days after the eggs have been laid, and their metamorphosis usually takes three to four months. Sometimes, however, they hibernate in water as tadpoles and do not develop further until the following spring. In this case they reach an abnormal length of about 17 cm.

The Common Spadefoot can be kept in a cool aquaterrarium containing a deep layer of sand or peat.

LENGTH:
5—8 cm.
BREEDING SEASON:
March and April; tadpoles metamorphose in June and July, sometimes in the following spring.

1 — adult frog
2 — string of eggs
3 — tadpoles
4 — large tadpole after hibernation

Eastern Spadefoot
(Syrian Spadefoot)
Pelobates syriacus

Pelobatidae

Natterjack Toad
Bufo calamita

Bufonidae

A robust spadefoot with a greyish back and with conspicuous blackish-brown spots which sometimes fuse into a reticular pattern. Sparsely scattered dermal tubercles have orange tips. The belly is uniformly greyish-white.

From south-western Asia it penetrates to Europe on the Balkan Peninsula, ranging up to the Rumanian Carpathians in the north. It occurs mostly in sandy regions. It is a nocturnal frog and its pupils contract to a vertical slit. During the day it lies buried in the soil but emerges at night to hunt worms, molluscs and other invertebrates. It breeds in water early in spring, and the tadpoles continue to live in water for 3—4 months.

It may be kept in a sandy vivarium provided with vegetation and a container for water.

The Natterjack Toad is characterized by a light band of wartless skin running along the middle of its olive-coloured back. Having very short limbs, it does not jump but walks on the ground. It lives almost all over Europe and prefers sunny but damp places with sandy soil in which it can quickly bury itself. In the twilight it goes hunting insects, worms and slugs.

It should be kept in a semi-desert vivarium with a dish of water, or in an aquaterrarium provided with a water-filled pan.

Pelobates syriacus:
LENGTH:
7—7.5 cm.
BREEDING SEASON:
March and April; tadpoles metamorphose in July to September.

Bufo calamita:
LENGTH:
7—8 cm.
BREEDING SEASON:
March to May; tadpoles metamorphose in June and July.

1 — *Pelobates syriacus*
2 — *Bufo calamita* — adult
3 — *Bufo calamita* — tadpoles

Common Toad

Bufo bufo

The Common Toad is a powerfully built animal with a massive, broad head. The ground colour is grey or brown to brownish-black and the back and flanks are covered with abundant tubercles. The belly is yellowish or dirty white-grey, and the eyes are copper-coloured. Two large crescent-shaped glands which secrete an irritating exudation are located behind the head. Males are usually substantially smaller than females.

The Common Toad is found all over Europe, both in lowlands and mountains. It lives in fields, gardens, parks, meadows, and frequently even in human settlements. The adults are active in the evening or by night, when they hunt slugs, earthworms and arthropods which they consume in large quantities. They leave their underground winter shelters at the beginning of March and make for water to mate. The female lays her eggs in strings, 3—5 metres long, which she coils about water plants. The newly-hatched tadpoles are very small, measuring only about 0.5 cm. Their metamorphosis takes about four months. Several subspecies exist in Europe.

It can be kept in a semi-desert vivarium with a small water container, or in an aquaterrarium.

LENGTH:
males 8 cm,
females 13 cm.
BREEDING SEASON:
March;
tadpoles
metamorphose in
June and July.

1 — string of eggs
2-3 — tadpoles
4-5 — adults

Green Toad

Bufo viridis

A variegated toad whose ground colour is grey or greenish. On its back, sides and legs there are conspicuous, well-defined dark-green spots. The belly is a uniform light green, rarely marked with dark dots. The skin is smoother than in the Common Toad; the tubercles on the back do not stand out so markedly and are, here and there, brick-red. The coloration is more contrasting in females than in males.

It is distributed from central and southern Europe to eastern Asia and North Africa where it inhabits lowlands and mountains but avoids densely wooded regions. Occasionally, it is abundant also in city parks, gardens and housing estates. Slightly over 1,000 metres is the highest altitude reached by this toad in central Europe, while in the south it can reach 2,000 metres. It is active in the daytime as well as at night. Compared with the Common Toad, it is more slender and has longer legs, features which enable it to move more swiftly. The adults may often be found far away from water. Their diet includes worms, insects and slugs. They hibernate in holes in the earth, under fallen logs, stones, etc. They leave their shelters in April and breed a short time afterwards.

The Green Toad can be kept in a semi-desert vivarium with a dish of water.

LENGTH:
10 cm.
BREEDING SEASON:
April;
tadpoles
metamorphose in
June and July.

1 — eggs with tadpoles
2-3 — adults

Common Tree Frog

Hylidae

(Green Tree Frog)

Hyla arborea

A slender, broad-headed frog whose digits end in suction discs. A dark lateral streak, edged with white above, runs along each side of the body. The skin is grass-green and smooth on the back, pale grey and finely granulated on the belly. The male has a vocal sac on his throat which inflates into the shape of a large bladder when he is croaking.

It lives in the temperate zone of Europe and Asia as well as in north-western Africa, moist areas with lush vegetation being its favourite habitat. While in spring it keeps close to water, in summer and autumn it prefers to stay on shrubs and trees where it is an excellent climber thanks to the suction pads on its digits. Its perfect camouflage makes it invisible against the tree foliage: it can quickly change its colour from green to greyish or even to brown. Small insects and spiders are its favourite food. Mating takes place in spring and the females lay their eggs in small clusters. Newly metamorphosed individuals are 15—20 mm long.

Southern Europe is the habitat of the closely allied Stripeless Tree Frog *(Hyla meridionalis)* which, in contrast to the Common Tree Frog, has no dark lateral bands along its sides.

Both these species may be kept in a warm aquaterrarium. Their assumed value as weather prophets is mere superstition.

LENGTH:
5 cm.
BREEDING SEASON:
April to June; tadpoles metamorphose in August and September.

1-2 — adults
3 — eggs
4 — tadpole

Common Frog

Rana temporaria

This frog's back is brown and usually dark-spotted; its dirty-white belly bears greyish-brown spots. A light longitudinal streak may run along the centre of the back and a dark blotch extends behind the eyes to the fore limbs. It differs from the Moor Frog in having a rounded head and obtuse snout. Its hind legs are shorter than those of other true frogs.

The area of distribution of the Common Frog is discontinuous, being divided into two distinct areas. The western part covers central and northern Europe, and the eastern part covers the Far East, north-eastern China and northern Japan. It inhabits woods, fields, meadows and peat-bogs — always in a moist environment near water. In southern regions it prefers foothill and mountain regions, while in the north it occurs also in the lowlands. Its food consists of slugs and various arthropods. Large numbers of these frogs often gather in the mud at the bottom of ponds to hibernate. Mating takes place very early in spring, often at a time when the water surface is still partly covered with ice. The eggs usually float in large clusters on the water surface. After 2—3 months the tadpoles metamorphose into frogs.

The Common Frog can be kept in a relatively long aquaterrarium with a small water container.

LENGTH:
8—10 cm.
BREEDING SEASON:
March and April, but later in higher altitudes; tadpoles metamorphose in June and July.

1 — male and female in amplexus
2 — eggs
3 — newly hatched tadpoles
4 — tadpole

Agile Frog

(Dalmatian Frog)
Rana dalmatina

Moor Frog

(Field Frog)
Rana arvalis

The colour of the back of the Agile Frog usually varies from a uniform light brown to rose-brown. A conspicuous dark spot is situated between the eyes and fore limbs. Extraordinarily long hind legs allow it to make long leaps to a distance of as much as 2 metres.

It occurs throughout southern and central Europe and in north-western Asia and shows a liking for light, deciduous lowland woods. It returns to water only to mate. Earthworms, spiders and small insects constitute its diet. Females lay clusters of eggs early in spring. Towards the end of summer the tadpoles metamorphose into small froglets that reach maturity in 3—4 years.

The Moor Frog has a brown back and sides, often spotted with black. A relatively broad, light band runs along the centre of the back, edged on either side with narrow dark streaks. The front of the snout is long and pointed and a dark patch can be seen behind each eye. It resembles the Common Frog.

Its home is in central and northern Europe where it lives in lowlands up to an elevation of about 600 metres, in peaty and swampy districts. It feeds on various arthropods and slugs. It breeds in spring and the tadpoles metamorphose in summer into little frogs about 1 cm in length; these take 3 years to mature.

Both species may be kept in a large, long, cold aquaterrarium with a small container of water.

Rana dalmatina:
LENGTH:
7—9 cm.
BREEDING SEASON:
March and April;
tadpoles
metamorphose in
August.

Rana arvalis:
LENGTH:
6—7.5 cm.
BREEDING SEASON:
March to May;
tadpoles
metamorphose in
July and August.

1 — *Rana
dalmatina*
2 — *Rana
dalmatina*
— tadpole
3 — *Rana arvalis*

Edible Frog
Rana esculenta

Ranidae

A frog having a grass-green or olive back usually marked with dark spots and frequently bearing a longitudinal yellowish-white dorsal band. The ventral parts are white or spotted with grey. The vocal sacs situated at both corners of the male's mouth are whitish or yellowish. This frog lacks the dark temporal spots. The skin is smooth or slightly warty. The females are larger than the males.

The Edible Frog occurs over the whole of Europe, except on the Iberian Peninsula and the Balkans, and is abundant particularly at lower and medium elevations. Of all true frogs, it is best adapted to aquatic life. It stays on the banks of rivers, ponds etc. and, when in danger, it quickly jumps into the water. Its diet is formed by various insects, worms, slugs, small fishes, tadpoles and even smaller frogs. It hibernates from October to April in the bottom mud though some young frogs do so under withered leaves at the water's edge. After mating in spring, the female deposits her eggs in small clusters in shallow water. Tadpoles metamorphose into 2 cm long froglets towards the end of summer or in autumn, depending on the temperature of water.

It can be kept in a large and long aquaterrarium containing a deeper water container.

LENGTH: Females 9—10 cm, exceptionally 12 cm, males 7.5 cm. BREEDING SEASON: May and June; tadpoles metamorphose from September to November.

Marsh Frog

(Croaking Frog)

Rana ridibunda

Ranidae

This large frog resembles the Edible Frog in co-loration. The vocal sacs of males, located at the corners of the mouth, vary from greyish to black. The skin is warty. Females exceed males in size.

Its range extends from northern, central and south-eastern Europe to the entire temperate zone of Asia, eastwards as far as Japan. It shows a preference for places near stagnant or sluggish, warm waters; in central and northern Europe it is found at lower elevations but in southern Europe also in mountains up to about 2,000 metres. It feeds on a wide variety of invertebrates and small vertebrates. In the fry ponds of fish farms, it can damage the young fish populations. It hibernates at the bottom of deeper waters and is active from April to October or November. It breeds in spring and 3 or 4 months later the tadpoles meta-morphose into minute froglets. In Europe, this frog occurs as two subspecies. It can successfully interbreed with the Edible Frog under natural conditions.

If kept in an artificial environment, it requires a large, cold aquaterrarium with a relatively ex-tensive and deep swimming pool.

LENGTH:
Females 12 cm, exceptionally 15 cm; males 9—10 cm.
BREEDING SEASON:
April and May; tadpoles meta-morphose in July and August.

Striped-neck Terrapin

Emydidae

(Caspian Terrapin)

Mauremys caspica (= Clemmys caspica)

The ground colour of the dorsal shield varies from olive-green to brown and bears a reticular pattern. The ventral shield is black or yellowish, spotted with black. Both the fore and the hind limbs are black with yellow or whitish longitudinal streaks. On either side of the neck there are yellow, pale-grey or orange stripes, and yellow ringed spots are present on the temples.

It is distributed throughout southern Europe, north-eastern Africa and the warm zone of western Asia where it lives in swiftly flowing, clean mountain brooks, but it can also be found in turbid and muddy pools in the lowlands. In daytime it likes to bask in the sun at the waterside; when in danger, it quickly disappears into the water. It hunts invertebrates and smaller vertebrates but also takes dead animals and vegetable food. After mating in spring or early summer, the female digs holes in the earth where she lays her 5—10 hard-shelled eggs. Incubation lasts some 70—100 days and the young are about 2 cm long on hatching.

This species can be kept in a warm aquaterrarium containing a large water-filled tank and branches submerged in water.

LENGTH:
20—30 cm.
EGG-LAYING
PERIOD:
June and July.
HIBERNATION
PERIOD:
November to March.

European Pond Terrapin
Emys orbicularis

Emydidae

The dorsal shield of this turtle is brown-green, green-black or black, spotted with yellow. Yellowish markings also cover the dark-coloured legs and head. The yellow plastron bears dark spots. The fore limbs have five webbed digits while the hind limbs have only four.

It has a wide distribution, being found from southern and central Europe to the northern parts of Africa and western Asia in pools, lakes, ox-bow lakes, sluggish rivers, brooks and swamps. It is fond of basking in sunny places at the water's edge and if danger threatens, it quickly dives below the surface. It is mainly carnivorous. Larger prey is torn with the aid of strong claws on the fore legs. It hibernates at the water bottom in mud and mates in spring; 4—6 weeks after mating, the female lays 3—12 round eggs in a hollow in the soil. The young, about 2 cm in length, hatch in August or September.

The European Pond Terrapin can be kept in a warm aquaterrarium with a larger water-filled container, or in an aquarium with shallow water and relatively large stones and branches showing above the surface. Like the Striped-neck Terrapin, it is fed with worms, insects, fish and amphibians.

LENGTH:
20—30 cm.
EGG-LAYING
PERIOD:
May and June.
HIBERNATION
PERIOD:
October to April
in more northerly
regions;
November to
March
in southern
Europe.

1 — adults
2 — eggs
3 — young

Hermann's Tortoise
Testudo hermanni

A terrestrial tortoise with an ivory-yellow to olive-green carapace marked with dark spots. There are two supracaudal plates above its tail which terminates in a strong horny scale. The thighs of the hind legs are smooth on their inner side.

Two subspecies occur in southern Europe and on the Mediterranean islands. Lowland areas covered with a dense growth of shrubs are its favourite habitat. It lives predominantly on plants and spends the winter under fallen leaves. It mates a short time after emerging from hibernation— usually in March. The female deposits 2—5 eggs in the soil and these hatch after about 10—12 weeks. The newly-emerged young are about 4 cm long.

Since it makes few demands on its breeders, this tortoise is a favourite for keeping not only in desert vivaria, but also in gardens or indoors in boxes. It is fed with vegetables, fruit and, from time to time, with meat. For the winter the animal should be placed in a cold cellar or outhouse, in a container filled with dry leaves and grass for bedding.

LENGTH: 20—25 cm.
EGG-LAYING PERIOD: April to June.
HIBERNATION PERIOD: November to February; in more northerly regions October to March.

Horsfield's Tortoise

Testudo horsfieldi

Spur-thighed Tortoise
(Grecian Tortoise)
Testudo graeca

Horsfield's Tortoise is a small terrestrial tortoise living in the lower Volga region, in Turkestan, Iran, Afghanistan and North Pakistan. Its carapace is markedly flat and the tail ends in a horny spike. It lives in steppe and semi-desert regions and in some places reaches considerable altitudes — over 1,200 metres above sea level. It survives the winter and the driest summer days in underground shelters. Mating time is in spring. Approximately two months later, the female lays 3 — 5 eggs that hatch in August. The newly-hatched young are 3 — 5 cm long.

The Spur-thighed Tortoise resembles Hermann's Tortoise in coloration, but it has only one supracaudal plate above the tail. The tail itself is rounded and has no horny spike at the tip. The insides of the thighs bear conspicuous horny projections.

It occurs in the low-lying shrubby areas of southern Europe, North Africa and south-western Asia. The biology of the Spur-thighed Tortoise is like that of Hermann's Tortoise.

These species can be kept either in a desert vivarium provided with vegetation, or freely in the garden. They should be given the same conditions for hibernation as Hermann's Tortoise.

Testudo horsfieldi:
LENGTH:
16 — 20 cm.
EGG-LAYING
PERIOD:
May and June.
HIBERNATION
PERIOD:
November to March;
often aestivates in dry summers.

Testudo graeca:
LENGTH:
25 — 30 cm.
EGG-LAYING
PERIOD:
May and June.
HIBERNATION
PERIOD:
November to March.

1 — *Testudo horsfieldi*
2 — *Testudo graeca*

Green Turtle
(Edible Turtle)
Chelonia mydas

Chelonidae

A huge green-brown to olive-coloured sea turtle with yellowish or brown spots and a yellow-white lower part. Each of its fin-like flippers has a single claw.

It is at home in all tropical and subtropical seas. Only rarely does it wander to the European shores of the Mediterranean and Atlantic. Unlike the other sea turtles it is predominantly herbivorous, its main food being sea-weeds. It mates several times a year; the spherical eggs, approximately 4 cm in diameter, are laid in holes dug by the female in the sandy shores of uninhabited islands. It takes the embryo 6—10 weeks to develop. After emerging from the sand, the hatchlings quickly follow the shortest route to the sea. Instinctively they find the right direction but many of them fall victim to birds and some of those that succeed in reaching water are caught by predatory fish.

From time to time, sea turtles of other species stray to European shores: the Loggerhead *(Caretta caretta)* which is about 1 metre in length; the smaller Tortoise-shell Turtle *(Eretmochelys imbricata)*; and the giant among the sea turtles, the Leather-back *(Dermochelys coriacea)*.

LENGTH:
140 cm.
EGG-LAYING
PERIOD:
2—5 batches each year containing 75—200 eggs.

1 — adult
2 — young

Kotschy's Naked-toed Gecko

Gekkonidae

Cyrtodactylus kotschyi (= Gymnodactylus kotschyi)

Turkish Gecko
Hemidactylus turcicus

Kotschy's Naked-toed Gecko has a grey or brown, often cross-barred back with small round and larger granulated scales; its belly is porcelain-white. The pupils contract to vertical slits. There are no suction pads on the tips of its fingers and toes.

It lives in southern Europe as well as in the temperate zone of western Asia, its favourite habitat being rock fissures, stone piles and buildings where it is often seen swiftly climbing along walls and ceilings. It is most active in the evening and by night, hunting insects and spiders. Towards the end of spring, the female deposits usually two eggs in various crevices; the young geckos hatch in summer.

In the Turkish Gecko, the ground colour of the back varies from greyish to brown and bears irregularly arranged dark spots. It can quickly change its colour in accordance with its surroundings. Two longitudinal rows of suction pads are located on the underside of the tips of its fingers and toes.

Its original habitat is the Mediterranean region but it has been accidentally carried by ship as far away as North America and Cuba. It seeks similar shelters as Kotschy's Naked-toed Gecko. It is capable of making relatively loud sounds.

Both these geckos can be kept in a semi-desert or desert vivarium which should contain hiding places and a small container of water.

Cyrtodactylus kotschyi:
LENGTH:
8—10 cm.
EGG-LAYING
PERIOD:
April and May.
HIBERNATION
PERIOD:
beginning of December to March.

Hemidactylus turcicus:
LENGTH:
8—10 cm.
EGG-LAYING
PERIOD:
April and May.
HIBERNATION
PERIOD:
November to March.

1 — *Cyrtodactylus kotschyi*
2 — *Hemidactylus turcicus*

Moorish Gecko

(Wall Gecko)

Tarentola mauritanica

This is the largest European gecko. It is able to change colour to blend with the surroundings and it also does so in response to changes in temperature. In full sunlight its colour is usually dark, becoming lighter in the evening. Its dorsal surface is often marked with bright cross-bands. On the underside of the digits there are transverse suctorial lamellae. The head is broad and the flattened body is covered with hook-like scales which are particularly conspicuous at the base of the tail.

It inhabits southern Europe, North Africa and the Mediterranean islands where it can be found on sunny rocks, walls, and under stones. In spring it leaves its shelter in the morning, but in summer not before the evening. It feeds on a variety of arthropods which it catches by leaping at them.

It breeds early in spring and lays its eggs in crevices and under stones. The young, which measure 3—5 cm, hatch after 3—4 months. Except in colder regions, it does not hibernate in winter.

It can be kept in a semi-desert vivarium containing branches and a water pan, at a temperature of 24—26° C, and should be fed with insects.

LENGTH:
14—16 cm.
EGG-LAYING
PERIOD:
April.
HIBERNATION
PERIOD:
in Europe,
December to end
of February; in
North Africa it
does not
hibernate.

1 — adult
2 — ventral side

Agama

(Sling-tailed Agama or Hardun)
Agama stellio

Caucasian Agama
Agama caucasica

The Agama is a large-sized member of the family and is extremely variable in colour. The back is usually black-brown or yellow-brown and the tail is cross-barred with alternating yellow and brown bands. The scales are spiny and in adult males they are frequently spotted with blue.

It is found on eastern Mediterranean islands, in north-eastern Africa and in Turkey, spending most of its time in dry, sunny places near rocks, old walls and trees. It is very nimble and shy. Its food consists mainly of various invertebrates and small vertebrates but sometimes it also eats fruit.

In early summer the female lays 8—14 eggs under stones or in rock crevices. When they hatch in August or September, the young are about 4 cm long.

The Caucasian Agama lives in Transcaucasia, in northern Turkey and in the warm regions of western India. It resembles the Agama in shape, size and habits. Frequently it gathers in great numbers to sun on the rocks.

Both species may be kept in a desert vivarium containing stones for shelter. They should be fed with various insects.

Agama stellio:
LENGTH:
30—40 cm.
EGG-LAYING
PERIOD:
June.
HIBERNATION
PERIOD:
December to
January.

Agama caucasica:
LENGTH:
25—30 cm.
EGG-LAYING
PERIOD:
May and June.
HIBERNATION
PERIOD:
December to
March.

1 — *Agama stellio*
2 — *Agama caucasica*

European Toad-headed Agama

Phrynocephalus helioscopus

Agamidae

A small grey or brown agama whose back is usually adorned with cross-bands varying from dark-brown to black. On its throat there are two red spots with blue margins. The head is broad and depressed from above, the body is short and stout. The tail in males is ringed with dark bars, its base is thickened and the tip is red.

This toad-headed agama is found in northern Iran, in Turkey and in the Middle East; in Europe, its range extends to the lower Volga basin and to Transcaucasia. It inhabits dry steppe and rocky areas where vegetation is scarce. The food of this small agama consists mainly of ants, beetles and other insects, as well as their larvae.

During hibernation it finds shelter under stones and in rock crevices which it leaves usually in March. In spring the female lays a clutch containing 2—5 eggs, and often does so repeatedly.

It can be kept in a desert vivarium containing sand and stones and maintained at a temperature of 25—30° C. It should be fed with small insects.

LENGTH:
10—12 cm.
EGG-LAYING
PERIOD:
May;
frequently several
clutches are laid.
HIBERNATION
PERIOD:
November to
March.

Mediterranean Chameleon

(Common Chameleon)

Chamaeleo chamaeleon

An arboreal species whose body is laterally flattened. The head is distinct from the body and, at its rear, there is a characteristic helmet-like crest. The bulging eyes can move independently of each other. The legs are adapted to climbing along branches: they form a kind of clasping tongs produced by the fusion of digits. This chameleon has a prehensile tail and a long protrusible tongue which terminates in a mobile digit-like projection.

It lives in North Africa, western Asia, and on Mediterranean islands (for example Crete). On the European continent it ranges to southern Spain and Portugal. It stays on trees and shrubs where its coloration enables it to merge perfectly with the surroundings. The chameleon's ability to change colour is proverbial. Its movements are sluggish and it uses its long, sticky tongue to catch its prey which is composed mostly of insects.

Two months after mating—which takes place in late summer and in autumn—the female deposits about 30 elongate eggs in a small hollow in the earth. The young emerge in the following summer.

The European Chameleon may be kept in a semi-desert vivarium at a temperature of 24—28° C. Branches on which it can climb should be provided.

LENGTH:
25—30 cm.
EGG-LAYING
PERIOD:
November to December.
HIBERNATION
PERIOD:
in colder regions January and February, in subterranean shelters; in warm regions it does not hibernate.

Ocellated Skink

Scincidae

(Cylindrical Skink)
Chalcides ocellatus

A yellow-brown to green-grey skink whose back is scattered with longitudinal rows of small dark spots each of which has a white dot in its middle. The belly is porcelain-white. The whole body is covered with smooth, glossy scales. Each of the short and strong limbs has five digits. The head and the base of the tail merge without clear delineation into the cylindrical body.

It occurs in North Africa and western Asia and extends to Mediterranean areas overgrown with thorny shrubs (maquis) in Greece, Sicily and Sardinia. It favours warm, sunny, sheltered places and takes refuge under stones or entirely buries itself in the sand. A large variety of invertebrates, particularly insects, constitute its diet.

It mates soon after emerging from hibernation in March and the female gives birth to 6—15 young towards the beginning of summer.

The Ocellated Skink may be kept in a desert vivarium with a layer of sand at the bottom, a container of water, flat stones and pieces of tree bark.

LENGTH:
18—20 cm.
TIME OF BEARING YOUNG:
May to July.
HIBERNATION PERIOD:
December to March;
it does not hibernate in warm regions.

Balkan Wall Lizard
(Grass Lizard)
Podarcis taurica (= Lacerta taurica)

Snake-eyed Skink
(Balkan Lidless Skink)
Ablepharus kitaibelii

The Balkan Wall Lizard is a variegated lizard with a short, slightly pointed head and a relatively long, narrow tail. It is abundant in southern parts of the European territory of the USSR and on the Balkan Peninsula, ranging northwards as far as Hungary and Rumania. Steppe localities overgrown with grasses and low shrubs are its usual habitat. It feeds on small insects. The female lays 2—6 eggs towards the end of spring and the young hatch in the summer.

The Snake-eyed Skink is a slender animal with a lustrous dorsal surface varying from greyish to brown-red. Two broad, dark streaks run along the sides of the body. The belly is grey-white, the legs are short, and the distance between fore legs and hind legs is relatively great. The tail is very long.

It is distributed throughout western Asia and penetrates into Europe on the Balkan Peninsula. Northwards it reaches the southern parts of Czechoslovakia. It lives on dry, stony slopes, frequently under oaks. In the daytime it keeps hidden under the stones but after nightfall it goes out hunting small insects on which it lives. Unlike most skinks, it is viviparous.

Both these species can be kept in a semi-desert vivarium containing grass turfs and a container of water, maintained at a temperature of 22—30° C.

Podarcis taurica:
LENGTH:
15—18 cm.
EGG-LAYING
PERIOD:
May and June.
HIBERNATION
PERIOD:
December to
February.

Ablepharus kitaibelii:
LENGTH:
10—11 cm.
EGG-LAYING
PERIOD:
May and June.
HIBERNATION
PERIOD:
in northern
regions November
to March, in the
south December
to February.

1 — *Podarcis taurica*
2 — *Ablepharus kitaibelii*

Sand Lizard
Lacerta agilis

Lacertidae

The coloration of this species is highly variable. The brownish or grey-brown back and sides are usually strewn with dark circular patches which have whitish centres. In spring and summer, the sides of the male's body are grass-green and sometimes the back assumes a green colour, while in the females brownish hues predominate. Sometimes the back of either sex may be brown or red.

It is distributed throughout Europe as well as in western and central Asia and inhabits both lowlands and hilly regions. It prefers sunny, sheltered places at the edge of woods and meadows, slopes covered with grass or shrubs, wasteland and old quarries; it is also plentiful in gardens and parks. The Sand Lizard's diet consists of locusts, flies, beetles, spiders and other arthropods. It spends the winter underground. Towards the end of spring or at the beginning of summer the female lays 5—15 longish eggs, provided with a leathery cover, in a shallow hole in the earth. In about 6—8 weeks, the young lizards measuring 3—4 cm hatch out. There are many subspecies.

It can be kept in an unheated semi-desert vivarium and requires a hibernation period.

LENGTH:
16—20 cm.
EGG-LAYING
PERIOD:
May and June.
HIBERNATION
PERIOD:
October to end of
March.

1 — female
2 — male
3 — the red-
backed form
4 — eggs
5 — young

Viviparous Lizard

Lacerta vivipara

Lacertidae

The back of this lizard varies in colour from grey-brown to dark brown; a slightly darker streak may run along the spine and is flanked by an even darker discontinuous stripe. A continuous dark band bordered by light-coloured spots appears on either side of the body. The belly is yellowish or grey in females; in males it varies from yolk yellow to orange, spotted with black. The tail is relatively short and thick.

It occurs throughout Europe and Asia—in damp places at high elevations, to 3,000 metres, and in the north even on low-lying land. Its movements are relatively sluggish and it spends the hibernation period in underground shelters, usually in very deep burrows. Mating takes place in May or June and three months afterwards the female gives birth to 3—10 young measuring 3 cm. The viviparity of this species is a mode of adaptation to a cold living environment: in the lower altitudes of southern Europe it is sometimes oviparous. It feeds mostly on small insects.

It can be kept in a cool, semi-desert vivarium at a temperature of 15—20° C.

LENGTH
15—16 cm.
TIME OF BEARING YOUNG:
August and September.
HIBERNATION PERIOD:
September, October to March, April, according to locality; in warmer regions it remains active throughout the winter.

1 — male
2 — female
3 — young
4 — eggs with hatching young

Wall Lizard
Podarcis muralis (= Lacerta muralis)

Lacertidae

A slender lizard with a flat, pointed head and a narrow tail which is almost twice as long as the rest of the body. Its grey-brown back bears dark spots or a dark reticular pattern. In females the spots are frequently joined up into rows, forming a dark band bordered on either side by lighter streaks. The flanks also have conspicuous rows of dark patches. In males, blue spots are present between the sides and belly.

Its habitats are sunny, stony areas of southern and central Europe and Asia Minor. It can run amazingly quickly and is an excellent rock climber. Various arthropods, particularly insects, provide the main source of its food. Two or three times a year the female deposits her 2—8 eggs in a little hole dug in the soil. On hatching two months later the young are 2—3 cm long. In Europe, especially on the Mediterranean islands, it exists as several subspecies.

It can be kept in a semi-desert or desert vivarium which must contain a pan of water and also stones and turfs. The temperature should be 25—30° C.

LENGTH:
18—25 cm.
EGG-LAYING
PERIOD:
May to July (two or three times).
HIBERNATION
PERIOD:
in central Europe November to March, in southern Europe it remains active throughout the year.

1 — female
2 — male

Erhard's Wall Lizard

(Aegean Lizard)

Podarcis erhardi (= Lacerta erhardi)

This species resembles the Wall Lizard but for its back, which ranges from brownish to reddish-grey with a black and white pattern as well as two rows of large dark spots gradually decreasing in size towards the tail. The dark reticular markings on either side of the body may occasionally fuse to form a longitudinal streak. A row of blue spots runs along the outer margin of the belly. In males the belly is a vermillion orange, in females it is whitish.

This lizard inhabits dry, stony areas with scarce vegetation in the southern parts of the Balkans and the Aegean Islands. It is particularly fond of basking in sunny places — on dry walls, rocks, and piles of gravel. It is a very swift runner and an excellent climber. Its food consists of arthropods, particularly insects. It mates in spring, lays eggs at the beginning of summer, and the newly hatched young, measuring about 3 cm, appear in September. The Aegean Islands are inhabited by several geographical races that differ in coloration, pattern and arrangement of the dark spots on the back and sides of the body.

Erhard's Wall Lizard can be kept in a desert or semi-desert vivarium provided with stones and turfs; the water in the container should be changed frequently.

LENGTH:
18—22 cm.
EGG-LAYING
PERIOD:
May and June.
HIBERNATION
PERIOD:
January and
February in cold
winters only;
otherwise it
remains active
throughout the
year.

Green Lizard
Lacerta viridis

The grass-green back of the male is densely covered with small black spots. The females' upper surface is brown-green, the young are brownish, sometimes marked with longitudinal streaks. In the breeding season, the throat in males is bright blue. The ventral side is yellow-white or yellow. The tail is twice the length of the rest of the body.

It occurs at lower elevations in central and southern Europe and Asia Minor; in the southernmost parts of its range, it may be found in mountainous regions up to 1,700 metres. It prefers dry places overgrown with shrubs but is also abundant in light, sunny woods, at field edges and in vineyards. Insects, small lizards and rodents are its chief food.

It usually mates in April, soon after coming out of hibernation, and between late May and July the female lays 6—20 eggs; the young that hatch 6—8 weeks later are 4 cm in length. Several subspecies of the Green Lizard occur in the Balkans and on some Mediterranean islands.

It can be kept in a semi-desert vivarium furnished with branches, shelters built of stones and a container of water.

LENGTH:
30—50 cm.
EGG-LAYING
PERIOD:
end of May to July.
HIBERNATION
PERIOD:
depends on the climate; in central Europe end of October to April.

1 — male
2 — female
3 — young

Balkan Green Lizard

(Three-lined Emerald Lizard)
Lacerta trilineata

A large lizard resembling the Green Lizard in coloration and shape of body. In males the back and sides are grass-green, scattered with dark dots. The head is decorated with a bluish-green reticular pattern and the throat is green. In females the upper part is either uniform green or marked with three to five narrow, yellow-white longitudinal streaks and the throat is yellow. The young are brownish with broad pale yellow longitudinal streaks on the back and sides.

It ranges from the Balkans and the adjacent Mediterranean islands to the western parts·of Asia, mostly inhabiting sunny lowlands; only exceptionally does it reach an altitude of 1,000 metres above sea level. Its food consists of various insects and small vertebrates. It is extremely agile. When exposed to danger, the adults flee to the tops of shrubs and trees, while the young lizards hide on the ground among leaves, under stones, etc. It mates in spring, lays 5—15 eggs and the young hatch between the middle of July and the end of August.

It can be kept in a semi-desert vivarium arranged in the same way as for the Green Lizard.

LENGTH:
40—50 cm.
EGG-LAYING
PERIOD:
May to July.
HIBERNATION
PERIOD:
in the north
November to
March;
in the south it is
active all the year
round, except in
rainy and cool
periods.

1 — adult
2 — young

Ocellated Lizard

Lacertidae

(Jewelled Lizard or Eyed Lizard)
Lacerta lepida

This species is the giant among European lizards and is extremely variable in colour. Typically, its back and sides are green-brown, but can sometimes be even brownish-red. Small black spots may fuse to form a reticular pattern. Both sides are marked with distinct azure-blue spots edged with black. The tail is relatively short, the body stout and the legs strongly developed for digging. The head is relatively large and broad, particularly in males.

Its range is limited to the south-western parts of Europe and to north-western Africa. It lives in lowlands as well as at higher elevations, preferring sunny places with plenty of shelters. It is very agile; when in danger it quickly disappears under a stone, into a rock crevice or up a tree. If picked up without due care, it may bite painfully. This lizard feeds on various invertebrates and small vertebrates. It mates towards the end of spring; the young, 5—6 cm in size, hatch three months after the eggs have been laid.

It can be kept in a desert vivarium provided with stones, turfs and a water container. The tank must be big enough to accommodate this relatively large lizard.

LENGTH:
70—90 cm.
EGG-LAYING
PERIOD:
April and May.
HIBERNATION
PERIOD:
October to
beginning of
March;
in North Africa it
does not usually
hibernate.

Italian Wall Lizard

(Sicilian Lizard or Ruin Lizard)
Podarcis sicula (= Lacerta sicula)

Mosor Rock Lizard

(Dalmatian Lizard)
Lacerta mosorensis

The Italian Wall Lizard's back and sides are marked with longitudinal rows of dark spots. In males the ground colour is greenish, in females brownish-grey. The tail is often twice the length of the rest of the body.

It occurs in the western parts of the Balkan Peninsula, in Italy, on some Mediterranean islands, and has also been introduced to Spain and even to the southern parts of the USA. It is very agile, and can be found in abundance from the lowlands up to 1,200 metres above sea level. It feeds on insects and succulent fruit. In summer the female lays 4—8 eggs; hatchlings measuring 4—5 cm appear six weeks later.

The Mosor Rock Lizard is distinctive due to the conspicuous longitudinal rows of small blue shields which run along its body sides. It is found in the karst regions of Dalmatia, Herzegovina and Montenegro at higher elevations—up to 1,500 metres. It prefers sunny, stony slopes and scree. Its diet consists of insects. The female lays 4—6 eggs under stones and in the soil.

A semi-desert vivarium containing stones, turfs and a dish of water is suitable for both these lizards; the Italian Wall Lizard requires a higher temperature (26—35° C), while the Mosor Rock Lizard is satisfied with a temperature of 25° C.

Podarcis sicula:
LENGTH:
20—25 cm.
EGG-LAYING
PERIOD:
July and August.
HIBERNATION
PERIOD:
January and February; on sunny days it leaves its shelter even in winter.

Lacerta mosorensis:
LENGTH:
15—20 cm.
EGG-LAYING
PERIOD:
July and August.
HIBERNATION
PERIOD:
November to April.

1— *Podarcis sicula*
2 — *Lacerta mosorensis*

Sharp-snouted Rock Lizard

(Sharp-headed Lizard or Karst Lizard)
Podarcis oxycephala (= Lacerta oxycephala)

Dalmatian Wall Lizard

(Adriatic Lizard)
Podarcis melisellensis (= Lacerta melisellensis)

The Sharp-snouted Rock Lizard's back varies from blue-grey to black-brown and bears a network of dark spots. The tail has alternating pale grey and black rings. The head is flattened and pointed and the tail is almost twice as long as the rest of the body.

It is restricted to the karst areas of Yugoslavia and the adjacent islands, from sea-level up to about 1,500 metres. It is very agile and climbs well on rocks and walls. Various insects are included in its diet. It comes out of hibernation towards the end of winter and mates in March or April. The young lizards are about 5 cm long when they hatch.

The ground colour of the Dalmatian Wall Lizard's back is usually olive-green to brown, but sometimes it can even be copper-coloured or almost black. The head is short, the snout is rounded and the tail is about twice the length of the rest of the body. It lives mainly in karst areas overgrown with low bushes, oaks and pines on the Balkan Peninsula and on Adriatic islands up to an altitude of 1,200 m. Its biology is similar to that of Erhard's Wall Lizard.

Both these species can be kept in a desert or semi-desert vivarium provided with turfs, stones and a water container.

Podarcis oxycephala:
LENGTH:
20 — 22 cm.
EGG-LAYING
PERIOD:
July.
HIBERNATION
PERIOD:
Not known.

Podarcis melisellensis:
LENGTH:
15 — 18 cm.
EGG-LAYING
PERIOD:
May and June.
HIBERNATION
PERIOD:
January and February.

1 — *Podarcis oxycephala*
2 — *Podarcis melisellensis*

Peloponnese Wall Lizard

Lacertidae

Podarcis peloponnesiaca (= Lacerta peloponnesiaca)

This lizard shows marked sexual dimorphism; in males the back is a bronze brown with a golden lustre, bordered on either side with a light longitudinal streak. A large turquoise-blue patch shows above the front legs. The outer row of ventral scales is blue, the belly of adult males is reddish. Females and the young are striped with black longitudinal bands along their yellowish-brown back, blue spots are absent, and the ventral side is white.

This little-known lizard is restricted to the Peloponnesian Peninsula. It occurs up to altitudes of 1,200 metres, on sandy slopes, in vineyards and in bushy areas. It is one of the most agile European lizards. It feeds on various insects, spiders and small vertebrates. Mating takes place early in spring and eggs are laid in the ground at the beginning of summer.

The Peloponnese Wall Lizard can be kept in a relatively large desert vivarium provided with shelters and a water container.

LENGTH: 22—25 cm, exceptionally 30 cm. EGG-LAYING PERIOD: May to July. HIBERNATION PERIOD: January and February.

1 — male
2 — female

Large Psammodromus

(Algerian Plated Lizard or Algerian Sand Racer)
Psammodromus algirus

Spanish Psammodromus

(Spanish Plated Lizard or Spanish Sand Racer)
Psammodromus hispanicus

The long and slender Large Psammodromus has a dark olive green or brown back and flanks. Two yellow, often dark-edged streaks run along each side of the body; a dark median dorsal band is usually present. The tail is twice the length of the rest of the body.

It occurs in southern France, on the Iberian Peninsula and in north-eastern Africa, and prefers sunny and dry, rocky districts and sometimes light woods or gardens. It is good at climbing shrubs and trees. When in danger, it rapidly buries itself in the sand and if attacked, it produces long, piping sounds. Its main food is made up of insects. In spring the female lays 8—11 eggs and the young hatch towards the end of summer.

When young, the Spanish Psammodromus is dark-brown with 4—6 light longitudinal streaks running along its back. The streaks tend to fade away as the animal grows older and the back usually becomes uniform in colour. Its tail is shorter than that of the Large Psammodromus. It lives on sand dunes almost barren of vegetation along the shores of Spain and southern France, and is a good digger.

Both these species can be kept in an arid or desert vivarium containing stones and branches, and maintained at a temperature of 25—32° C.

Psammodromus algirus:
LENGTH:
20—27 cm.
EGG-LAYING
PERIOD:
April.
HIBERNATION
PERIOD:
January and February, March.

Psammodromus hispanicus:
LENGTH:
10—12 cm.
EGG-LAYING
PERIOD:
April to June.
HIBERNATION
PERIOD:
December to March, depending on climatic conditions.

1 —
Psammodromus algirus
2 —
Psammodromus hispanicus

Dalmatian Algyroides
(Keeled Lizard)
Algyroides nigropunctatus

Lacertidae

Greek Algyroides
(Keeled Lizard)
Algyroides moreoticus

The Dalmatian Algyroides has a brown, olive-green or black-brown back strewn with small black dots. White spots are present on the sides. The dorsal scales are large and strongly keeled. The tail is about twice the length of the rest of the body.

It occurs in south-eastern Europe, particularly in damp localities, in lowlands where rocks, old walls and stone-piles are near at hand. It is very agile and shy. It hibernates under stones or underground. In spring it likes to bask in the sun all day long, often in great numbers, but in summer it spends the day in shelters which it leaves only in the mornings and evenings to hunt for various insects.

Closely related, but smaller in size, is the Greek Algyroides which inhabits the Peloponnese and some of the Ionian Islands. In its way of life it resembles the Dalmatian Algyroides.

Both these species can be kept in a semi-desert vivarium provided with a small rockery and a pan of water, and maintained at a temperature of about 30° C.

Algyroides nigropunctatus:
LENGTH:
15—20 cm.
EGG-LAYING
PERIOD:
April to June.
HIBERNATION
PERIOD:
December to end of February.

Algyroides moreoticus:
LENGTH:
10—13 cm.
EGG-LAYING
PERIOD:
April and May.
HIBERNATION
PERIOD:
January and February.

1 — *Algyroides moreoticus*
2 — *Algyroides nigropunctatus*

Slender Racer
Eremias velox

Steppe Racer
(Eremias or Desert Racer)
Eremias arguta

The Slender Racer has a grey or grey-green back with three black longitudinal streaks. Another black longitudinal band runs along each side of the body. This species is distributed from the northern coast of the Caspian Sea to Mongolia, where it is most often found in sandy steppes.

The Steppe Racer has a powerfully built brownish body adorned with longitudinal rows of light, dark-edged spots.

Its range extends from southern Rumania (the coastal area of Dobrogea) deep into central Asia. The places it inhabits are similar in character to those inhabited by the Slender Racer. It is extremely nimble and when danger threatens it quickly disappears into various crevices and other shelters, or rapidly covers itself with sand. Mating takes place in April, and in May the female lays 4—12 eggs. The young hatch in June. A second clutch of eggs is often laid in late summer. The diet of both these lizards consists of spiders and ants.

Both species can be kept in a desert vivarium provided with a sufficiently high layer of clean, fine sand and stones, and maintained at a temperature of 28—35° C. It is necessary to lower the temperature during the night.

Eremias velox:
LENGTH:
18—20 cm.
EGG-LAYING
PERIOD:
May (the second clutch in July or August).
HIBERNATION
PERIOD:
November to March.

Eremias arguta:
LENGTH:
15—18 cm.
EGG-LAYING
PERIOD:
May (the second clutch in July or August).
HIBERNATION
PERIOD:
November to March.

1 — *Eremias velox*
2 — *Eremias arguta*

Slow-worm
Anguis fragilis

Anguidae

This is a legless lizard with a grey, brown or olive green upper surface; a dark central dorsal band is present in females and in the young. In old males, azure-blue scales are sometimes scattered on the back and sides among the normally coloured ones.

It is distributed almost throughout the whole of Europe (northwards up to southern Sweden and Finland), in south-western Asia and north-western Africa. It is found in lowlands as well as mountains and it lives under fallen leaves, logs, stones, and in crevices. Its diet consists of earthworms, slugs and insect larvae, which it hunts both underground and on the surface. Like the other lizards, it can shed its tail when in danger.

It frequently stays in its underground winter shelters until April. The breeding season starts a short time afterwards. At the beginning of summer, the female bears 8—20 young. These are wrapped at birth in a transparent membrane which breaks almost immediately. There are several subspecies.

It can be kept in a semi-desert vivarium with mosses and flat stones which must be sprinkled with water every day. The temperature should be 18—26° C.

LENGTH:
40—45 cm.
TIME OF BEARING YOUNG:
June and July.
HIBERNATION PERIOD:
November to March, April.

1 — female
2 — male — specimen with blue scales

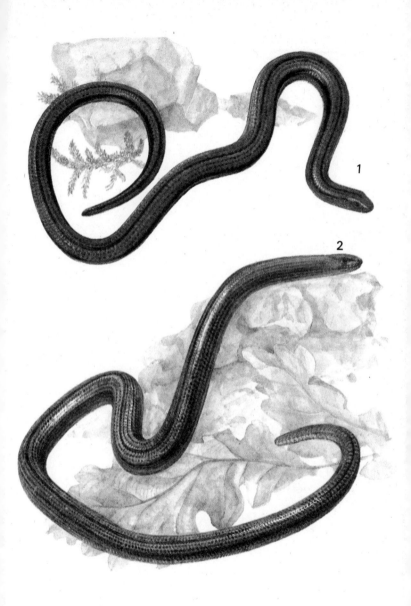

1

2

European Glass Lizard
(Scheltopusik or Glass Snake)
Ophisaurus apodus

Anguidae

This is a big legless lizard with a cylindrical body whose back is coloured brownish-red or brownish-yellow. Along both sides, a deep cutaneous groove runs from the auditory orifice to the anal opening. On either side of the anus there are two small outgrowths which are the vestiges of hind limbs. Beneath the scales there are osseous plates arranged in rings.

It occurs in south-eastern Europe, particularly in the Balkans, in north-eastern Africa and western Asia. Sunny lowlands, grassy slopes overgrown with shrubs and stony meadows are its habitat. It feeds on small vertebrates as well as on slugs, worms and other invertebrates. When it catches larger animals it rotates rapidly round its axis, thus stunning or killing its prey.

The European Glass Lizard hibernates underground. At the beginning of summer the female lays 6—10 elongate eggs from which, towards the end of August, longitudinally streaked or spotted young hatch out. It does not shed the upper skin layer in parts like the lizards but casts it off in one piece like the snakes.

It can be kept in a large, relatively long semi-desert vivarium at a temperature of 20—30° C and provided with a container of water and plenty of shelters.

LENGTH:
80—125 cm.
EGG-LAYING
PERIOD:
June and July.
HIBERNATION
PERIOD:
November to
March.

Sand Boa
(Spotted Sand Boa)
Eryx jaculus

Worm Snake
(Balkan Blind Snake)
Typhlops vermicularis

The Sand Boa is the only European representative of the family Boidae. It lives in steppe areas with scarce vegetation and in lowlands and hilly districts of south-eastern Europe, western Asia and North Africa. It is most often found under stones and in soft soil in which it can quickly bury itself. After dusk it leaves its shelter to hunt voles, lizards and other small vertebrates, coiling around them and suffocating them in the loops of its body. It mates early in spring, and towards the end of August the female gives birth to 6—18 young.

The Worm Snake is a small subterranean snake with smooth, glossy scales. Its back is flesh pink, and its belly and sides vary from yellowish to white. The head is not distinct from the body, the mouth is on the underside of the head and the eyes are minute. The rounded tail terminates in a short spine. It occurs in south-eastern Asia and in the southern parts of the Balkan Peninsula. It feeds on small invertebrates and is particularly fond of ants' eggs. In summer the female lays about 8 eggs.

Both the Sand Boa and the Worm Snake can be kept in a semi-desert vivarium with a water container and a deep layer of sand. The temperature should be 25—30° C. For the Worm Snake large flat stones and pieces of bark should be included.

Eryx jaculus:
LENGTH:
50—70 cm, rarely 80 cm.
TIME OF BEARING YOUNG:
August.
HIBERNATION PERIOD:
November to end of February.

Typhlops vermicularis:
LENGTH:
30—35 cm.
EGG-LAYING PERIOD:
May and June.
HIBERNATION PERIOD:
December to March.

1 — *Eryx jaculus*
2 — *Typhlops vermicularis*

1

2

Large Whip Snake
Coluber jugularis

This is the longest European snake. The back is an olive green, brown or black, and the scales are dark-edged both above and below with a yellow streak through the centre; these streaks are aligned in longitudinal rows. The head is spotted and streaked on its upper surface. The underside of the body is ochre-yellow or reddish-yellow.

It lives in steppes or on the bushy slopes of south-eastern Europe and western Asia. It is a typical diurnal snake and is capable of climbing shrubs. Its food consists of rodents, birds, lizards, snakes and insects. After nightfall it hides in rock fissures or in rodents' lairs.

Mating takes place early in spring, then in summer the female lays 7—20 eggs among leaves or in holes in the soil. The young measure approximately 25 cm on hatching. This snake is represented in Europe by two subspecies.

It can be kept in a semi-desert vivarium furnished with strong, stiff-leaved plants and several large stones.

LENGTH: 150—250 cm, exceptionally 250 cm.
EGG-LAYING PERIOD: June and July.
HIBERNATION PERIOD: November to March.

Balkan Whip Snake
Coluber gemonensis

Colubridae

This is a slender colubrid snake whose ground colour is grey-brown. The front part of the body is covered with dark and white spots which, further back, give way to longitudinal streaks. The underside is a uniform light or dark yellow. The head is small in relation to the body.

The Balkan Whip Snake inhabits south-eastern Europe, particularly the east Mediterranean regions, where it lives in dry, bushy areas as well as in light, sunny oak or pine forests. It spends most of its time on the ground but it can also climb shrubs. It is very agile and bites if attacked. Small vertebrates, such as mice, young birds, lizards and smaller snakes, as well as insects constitute its diet.

Mating takes place early in spring, 8—10 eggs are laid towards the end of summer or at the beginning of autumn. The newly-hatched young measure about 25 cm.

It can be kept in a warm (25—30° C) semi-desert vivarium furnished with shrub-like plants, stones and turfs. It is advisable to lower the temperature for the night.

LENGTH:
100—120 cm.
EGG-LAYING PERIOD:
June to beginning of September.
HIBERNATION PERIOD:
November to March.

Dahl's Whip Snake
(Slender Whip Snake)
Coluber najadum

Colubridae

This is a slender colubrid snake with a grey-brown or red-brown back, a light grey head and anterior part of the body, and a yellowish-white belly. On either side of the front part of the body, behind the head, there are oval-shaped, dark patches edged with light-yellow or white, decreasing in size from front to back.

It is distributed throughout south-eastern Europe, north-eastern Africa and south-western Asia, occurring in bushy areas near streams in both lowlands and highlands. It is extremely shy and swift. This species lives only on the ground and does not climb. It feeds almost exclusively on lizards, and only occasionally hunts locusts and other insects. If attacked, it secretes — like the Grass Snake — an unpleasantly smelling substance and defends itself by biting.

It rarely leaves its winter shelters before April. In summer it usually lays 3 — 5 eggs in rock crevices, hollows in the ground or under stones. The young measure 20 — 25 cm on hatching.

In the vivarium it requires a hiding-place among stones, shrub-like plants, a water pan, and a temperature of 25 — 30° C.

LENGTH:
110 — 120 cm.
EGG-LAYING
PERIOD:
June and July.
HIBERNATION
PERIOD:
October to April.

Western Whip Snake

(Green Whip Snake or Dark Whip Snake)
Coluber viridiflavus

The ground colour of this species is black; the yellow-green reticulation present on the front part of the body fuses to form longitudinal yellowish-green bars running along its rear part. The belly is yellow-grey, each ventral plate is dark-edged laterally.

It occurs in the regions bordering the western and central Mediterranean and reaches northwards as far as central France and southern Switzerland. Dry, rocky areas overgrown with low shrubs are its favourite habitat. It is one of the swiftest European snakes. If attacked, it immediately starts biting and then chews the wound. It is expert at climbing in shrubs and trees. Its main food comprises young birds, small mammals, lizards, snakes, and also insects and other invertebrates.

During mating, which occurs in spring, the male strongly grips the female with his teeth. In summer the female lays 8—10 oval eggs in the soil or under stones. The young hatch out in 6—8 weeks and measure about 25 cm. There are two European subspecies.

It can be kept in a warm, semi-desert vivarium.

LENGTH:
160—180 cm.
EGG-LAYING
PERIOD:
June to August.
HIBERNATION
PERIOD:
November to
March.

Smooth Snake
Coronella austriaca

Colubridae

This is a small, grey, brown or black-brown snake with two to four rows of dark markings, frequently confluent, extending along its back. On either side of the head a dark band runs from the nostrils to the throat, and there is another dark area at the back of the head. Because of these markings it is often mistaken for a viper but the spots are never arranged in the zigzag line characteristic of vipers; moreover, the Smooth Snake's head is much narrower than that of a viper and the whole body is much more slender.

It inhabits central and northern Europe, showing a preference for dry places abounding in stones and gravel. It is an exclusively diurnal snake. When young its diet is small lizards, but when older it hunts adult lizards, small mice, young snakes and Slow-worms. It coils in several loops around the captured prey, constricts and subsequently devours it. When attacked, it defends itself by vigorous biting.

Mating takes place early in spring; towards the end of summer the female gives birth to 2—12 young which emerge from the eggs at the moment of birth. Thus the Smooth Snake is ovoviviparous. The young are 13—18 cm long.

The Smooth Snake can be kept in a semi-desert vivarium containing stones.

LENGTH:
70—80 cm.
TIME OF BEARING
YOUNG:
August and
September.
HIBERNATION
PERIOD:
November to
March.

Aesculapian Snake
Elaphe longissima

Colubridae

This is a large colubrid snake with a light brown or dark brown back covered with white-flecked scales. The belly is white-yellow. In younger individuals, the rear part of the head may be marked with yellow or orange crescent-shaped areas, sometimes edged with black.

It is widespread throughout southern Europe and south-western Asia; in central Europe it occurs only in isolated populations, the most northerly of these being in Poland. It shows a preference for sunny, sheltered places in dry regions, especially on bushy and stony slopes in light and warm deciduous woods. It climbs expertly in trees and shrubs where it hunts birds, dormice and squirrels. Mice and voles, however, are the chief items of its diet. It kills prey by coiling around and constricting it.

Mating takes place in April and May; at the beginning of summer the female lays 5—8 eggs; the young hatch in September and measure about 20 cm. There are several subspecies in central and southern Europe.

It can be kept in a warm, semi-desert vivarium.

LENGTH:
180—200 cm.
EGG-LAYING
PERIOD:
June and July.
HIBERNATION
PERIOD:
end of October to
end of March.

1—adult
2—young

1

2

Leopard Snake

(Asia-Minor Chicken Snake)

Elaphe situla

Colubridae

This is one of the most colourful European snakes; the ground colour of its body varies from grey to light brown and the back is covered with large red or red-brown spots, edged with black, which extend from head to tail. The belly is usually pale in front and spotted with black in the rear, though sometimes it is blackish-brown or black.

It is distributed from southern Europe and south-western Asia eastwards as far as Asia Minor, the Caucasus and Crimea. It is common in dry, stony areas overgrown with thorny shrubs in which it climbs with great skill. Its food consists chiefly of mice and voles but it also hunts young birds and, less frequently, lizards. It resembles other chicken snakes in that it constricts its prey.

It is a warmth-loving snake, making for its winter shelters early in autumn and not leaving them before late spring. It mates in May; in summer the female lays 2—5 relatively large eggs under stones, among decaying leaves, or in the ground. The young are surprisingly large on hatching, measuring 30—35 cm; at first they live on young mice, voles and small lizards.

This species can be kept in a semi-desert vivarium, furnished with branches, at a temperature of 24—28° C.

LENGTH:
80—100 cm.
EGG-LAYING
PERIOD:
July.
HIBERNATION
PERIOD:
October to April.

Four-lined Snake

Elaphe quatuorlineata

Colubridae

This is a powerful colubrid snake with a brown dorsal surface marked by four black longitudinal streaks which fade away towards the tail. The young are spotted with dark brown or black. The underside is pale.

It is distributed throughout south-eastern Europe and the western parts of Asia where it lives on sunny hillsides, in light woods and at the edge of stagnant waters, frequenting rocky and bushy slopes. It is an agile climber in shrubs and trees where it hunts birds and raids their nests; it also feeds on various small mammals. It constricts its prey in the loops of its body.

It mates in spring and in summer the female lays 6—16 elongate eggs under stones and in soil crevices. The young hatch in September or October and are about 23 cm long. There are several subspecies.

It can be kept in a warm, semi-desert vivarium provided with branches.

LENGTH:
200—250 cm.
EGG-LAYING
PERIOD:
July and August.
HIBERNATION
PERIOD:
end of October to March.

Grass Snake
(Ringed Snake)
Natrix natrix

Colubridae

The back of this snake is coloured greyish-brown, sometimes with a bluish or greenish tinge, and may be decorated with four to six longitudinal rows of black spots which sometimes tend to fuse. The belly is yellow-white, checkered with black; in some individuals it may be completely black. At the back of the head there are two whitish or yolk-yellow crescent-shaped markings edged with black.

It is distributed throughout most of Europe, northwards as far as Scandinavia, in Asia as far as Siberia, and also in north-western Africa. It is a typical inhabitant of richly overgrown banks along stagnant and sluggish waters. Being an excellent swimmer, it can also skilfully hunt in water. When young it feeds on tadpoles and small frogs, but when older it prefers fish and especially adult amphibians, including toads.

It emerges from hibernation in March or April depending on the climatic conditions; it mates a short time afterwards, and in summer the female lays clusters of elongate, soft-shelled eggs among the decaying plant litter. Sometimes several females lay eggs in the same place. The newly-hatched young measure 15—20 cm. There are several subspecies.

It can be kept in a large semi-desert vivarium provided with a water-pool, or in an aquaterrarium.

LENGTH:
130—150 cm.
EGG-LAYING PERIOD:
July and August.
HIBERNATION PERIOD:
end of October to March or April.

Dice Snake
Colubridae

(Checkered Water Snake or Tessellated Snake)
Natrix tessellata

The ground colour of the body is grey to brown and the back and sides are marked with four to five rows of irregular dark spots which may fuse into longitudinal streaks. The belly varies from pale yellow to orange-red and is speckled with black. The head bears a forward-pointing, dark V-shaped patch.

The range of the Dice Snake extends from central and southern Europe deep into Asia, as far as north-western India and China. It lives near water, along banks overgrown with abundant vegetation. It swims even better than the Grass Snake and expertly catches fish and amphibians, consuming smaller prey in water but coming ashore with larger prey to devour it on dry land.

Mating takes place early in spring; in summer the female lays 5 — 20 oval eggs glued into clusters. The eggs hatch in 8 — 10 weeks and the newly-emerged young measure 12 — 15 cm. There is a large number of subspecies which differ greatly in colour.

Like the Grass Snake, it can be kept in a semi-desert vivarium containing a relatively large pool, or in an aquaterrarium.

LENGTH: 100 — 150 cm.
EGG-LAYING PERIOD: June to August.
HIBERNATION PERIOD: October to beginning of April.

Montpellier Snake
Malpolon monspessulanus

Colubridae

This is a stout colubrid snake with fangs located at the back of the upper jaw, below the eyes. Its colour varies from yellow to greyish-green or black; the dorsal and lateral regions bear many small black speckles which are completely or partly edged with yellow. These often join up to form five to seven longitudinal rows. The belly is a uniform yellow-grey, sometimes covered with spots. The skull is depressed between the eyes.

It occurs from southern Europe to western Asia and North Africa, living in sunny places overgrown with low shrubs and thorny vegetation, such as field edges, etc. It is a very alert and shy snake. Its diet is formed of small vertebrates — lizards, birds, mammals and snakes. Its venom is lethal to small prey, killing it within 3—5 minutes; the bite of a large individual may cause illness in man and the wound takes a long time to heal.

It hibernates in subterranean shelters, mates in April or May and eggs are laid by the female in summer. The young, 20—25 cm in length, hatch in September or October.

The Montpellier Snake can be kept in a desert vivarium containing turfs, stones, bushy vegetation and branches, and maintained at a temperature of 25—30° C.

LENGTH: 180—200 cm, exceptionally even more.
EGG-LAYING PERIOD: July and August.
HIBERNATION PERIOD: November to March.

European Cat Snake

Colubridae

Telescopus fallax

This is another back-fanged colubrid, the ground colour of which is light or dark grey with black markings on the back. The rear of the head bears a black patch; the sides of the body are adorned with black spots and the speckled belly is porcelain-coloured. The body is laterally flattened so that its height exceeds its breadth.

It is distributed both in the lowlands and in the hilly or mountainous districts of the Balkans, the Aegean region and the Near East. Dry, stony places overgrown with low shrubs in which it can climb are its preferred habitat. Because it becomes active after dark, its eyes are provided with vertical, slit-shaped pupils. It lives mostly on lizards but occasionally also captures small mammals. Before devouring its prey it coils around it and kills it by its venomous bite. However, its venom is not particularly dangerous for man.

Mating takes place in spring, and in summer the female lays 6—8 eggs under stones, in the ground or in rock fissures. The young are 15—20 cm long on hatching.

It can be kept in a desert vivarium furnished with stones and branches, and maintained at a temperature of 25—30° C.

LENGTH:
90—100 cm.
EGG-LAYING
PERIOD:
June to August.
HIBERNATION
PERIOD:
November to
March.

Nose-horned Viper

(Sand Viper or Horned Viper)
Vipera ammodytes

The ground colour of this species varies from light grey to reddish-brown or dark brown. A dark zigzag band, which, in males, is usually black, extends along the middle of the back. The body is wide and flattened. The typical broad, flat head is triangular in shape and the upper end of the snout bears a characteristic little horn. Hollow fangs are located at the front of the upper jaw.

It occurs in south-eastern and central Europe, the northern limit being Hungary and Austria; it is also found in the south-western parts of Asia. Its favourite spots are sunny places overgrown with bushy vegetation, rocky hillsides, stone piles, etc. It occurs at most altitudes.

Depending on the climate, it hibernates until February or April; mating takes place soon afterwards, and, in late summer or autumn, the female bears fully developed young measuring 15—20 cm. The first food of the young includes small lizards, shrews and small voles, while the adults hunt voles, mice, moles and small birds which they kill by striking them with their fangs. Its venom can be lethal to man.

It can be kept in a semi-desert vivarium containing stones and shrubs. A container of water should also be provided.

LENGTH:
90—100 cm.
TIME OF BEARING YOUNG:
August and September.
HIBERNATION PERIOD:
according to climatic conditions; October, November to February, April.

Adder
(Common Viper or Northern Viper)
Vipera berus

Viperidae

The coloration of this species is highly variable—from light grey or yellow-grey through various shades of brown to entirely black. The males are usually grey, the females brownish. A conspicuous broad and dark, zigzag band, indistinct in black forms, runs the full length of the back. When viewed from above, the broad head is triangular in shape and clearly distinct from the powerful body. Large fangs are located at the front of the upper jaw.

LENGTH: 75—90 cm. TIME OF BEARING YOUNG: June and July. HIBERNATION PERIOD: October, November to February, April.

Except in the extreme south, this species is distributed throughout Europe and ranges all the way across Asia to Japan; it inhabits lowlands as well as mountains where it occurs at considerable altitudes. It likes to bask in the sun on elevated places—stones, stumps, etc. The chief items of its diet are small mammals which it kills by striking them with lightning speed. It is shy and, unless accidentally disturbed, it shuns human beings. It sometimes bites in self-defence, however, and it is then necessary for the victim to see a doctor immediately as the venom is very strong indeed.

It hibernates in underground shelters, mates early in spring, and the female gives birth to 5—20 young, measuring 15—20 cm, at the beginning of summer.

It can be kept in a semi-desert vivarium and should be fed with white mice, like other vipers.

Asp Viper

Vipera aspis

This viper also has extremely variable coloration: light grey, brown, reddish-brown and orange-brown specimens have been recorded. The longer and more slender males bear a very dark dorsal pattern of cross-bars which sometimes form a zigzag or meandering line. Dark spots are also present on both sides of the body. The tip of the tail is orange. One of the characteristics of this species is the rounded snout.

It lives in southern and south-western Europe and ranges as far as Switzerland. Until recently its presence was reported even from the Schwarzwald. It inhabits both lowlands and mountains to altitudes of more than 2,500 metres above sea level, and prefers dry places such as in stone piles, abandoned quarries, etc.

It leaves its winter shelter in March or April and mating takes place a short time afterwards. Towards the end of summer the female bears 4—18 young, 18—20 cm long. The young snakes feed at first on small lizards and later on small mammals which are killed by the potent venom. There are several subspecies.

It can be kept in a semi-desert vivarium containing stones and branches.

LENGTH:
70—75 cm.
TIME OF BEARING YOUNG:
August and September.
HIBERNATION PERIOD:
October to March, April.

Blunt-nosed Viper

(Levant Viper)

Vipera lebetina

Viperidae

This is the largest European viper. Its ground colour varies from dirty white to dark grey and the whole body is speckled with blue and orange. The back is marked with two series of kidney-shaped, light brown or ochre-coloured spots with dark edges. The sides of the body are speckled. The males are more brightly-coloured than the females. The head, which is clearly delineated from the slender neck, is broad, the large venom glands forming conspicuous bulges at the hind end. At the tip of the tail there is a pointed spine, about 1 mm long.

It is widespread in the mountains of North Africa and in both central and western Asia, reaching Europe only on some islands in the eastern Mediterranean. It lives on rocks, under piles of stones, in old stone walls and along the densely overgrown banks of mountain streams that dry up in summer. It feeds chiefly on small mammals, birds and lizards which, before being swallowed, are killed by the extremely powerful venom which may even be fatal to man. It is oviparous in some parts of its range and ovoviviparous in others. The young measure 15—20 cm at birth.

It can be kept in a desert vivarium containing stones, branches and shrubs, and maintained at a temperature of 22—30° C.

LENGTH:
150—200 cm.
TIME OF BEARING YOUNG:
June and July.
HIBERNATION PERIOD:
November to March,
in warm regions January and February.

KEEPING AMPHIBIANS
AND REPTILES IN THE HOME

This book is intended to show the reader the interesting and colourful world of amphibians and reptiles. It shows something of where and how these animals live under natural conditions, the demands they make on their habitat, their food requirements and their breeding habits. It may awaken an interest in keeping some of these animals at home, so that you can admire their colour and beauty, and observe their interesting habits at close quarters. Just as a carefully kept aquarium can beautify your home, so also can a neatly arranged vivarium containing amphibians or reptiles.

European amphibians and reptiles can successfully be kept in tanks of three basic types: the aquaterrarium, the semi-desert vivarium and the desert vivarium.

The aquaterrarium is suitable for keeping the majority of European amphibians, aquatic turtles and some colubrid snakes. A relatively deep container of water occupies at least one half of the floor of the tank, while the rest is taken up by soil, adequate shelters, plants, etc. An aquaterrarium should be heated as required by a covered electric bulb, situated, if possible, well away from the plants.

The semi-desert vivarium is used for keeping most of the central European reptiles and many of the south European ones. The back is made up of bark with peat-moss (*Sphagnum*) pushed into its vrevices, which should be regularly sprinkled with water to maintain the required humidity level. Sometimes a small pan of water may also be provided. Heating is by means of a suspended electric bulb which is switched off for the night.

The desert vivarium is suitable for keeping desert and steppe animals as well as many south European xerophilous reptiles. Adequate temperature is usually obtained by means of an electric bulb, or rarely by a heating coil sunk into the bottom of the tank. A 5 — 10 cm layer of fluvial sand, washed and sterilized by heat, is placed on the floor and a dish of water must be provided to satisfy the needs of a number of reptiles; this should be changed regularly.

Animals which, under natural conditions, live in the tops of trees and bushes require a similar living environment even in the vivarium. Therefore it should be planted with suitable plants or, at least, furnished with dry branches or twigs on which the animals can climb. Burrowing animals need to have the bottom of their tank covered by a layer of clean sand deep enough to hide in.

Every animal needs a living area which it can defend against rivals. In natural conditions, the more mobile the animal, the

a

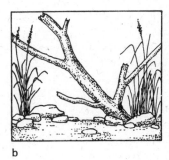
b

c

Fig. 11. Types of vivarium:
a) aquaterrarium,
b) semi-desert vivarium,
c) desert vivarium

larger is its territory. This fact should be respected by vivarium-keepers: animals must never be kept in tanks which are too small, neither should an excessively large number of individuals of the same species be made to live in a single larges-ized vivarium.

As with all other animals, the life of amphibians and reptiles is divided into periods of activity and those of rest. In diurnal animals, the period of activity sets in after daybreak and ends with the sunset, but for nocturnal animals the reverse is the case. The temperature is higher in the daytime than overnight—so it would be wrong to keep the temperature in the vivarium at the same level all the time. The variation of temperature between day and night has a most favourable effect on the animals, enabling them to have an adequate period of rest.

Seasonal temperature variations in the living environment are just as important as the diurnal rhytms mentioned above. These are most important for those amphibians and reptiles which inhabit temperate and cold geographical zones and which spend the cold season in a state of winter sleep, or hibernation. On the other hand animals from tropical regions, where long periods of rain alternate with periods of drought, spent the hottest and dryest season of the year in aestivation.

In many amphibians and reptiles, these periods are characterized by the slowing down of all active life processes. It is during these periods that the reproductive cells within their bodies are brought to full development. In many cases, the animals begin to pair and multiply as soon as they come out of hibernation and enter the period of full activity. The time of hibernation also affects the life span of animals: during their winter or summer sleep, all manifestations of life are reduced to the minimum and this contributes to the prolongation of life.

Appropriate feeding is of great importance for the animals' state of health and the duration of life. Most amphibians and reptiles are carnivorus, some species are omnivorous, still others are herbivorous. The feeding of carnivorous and insectivorous amphibians and reptiles in vivaria poses no problems if adequate supplies of various insects and small vertebrates can be provided. Problems, however, may arise when feeding herbivorous animals as knowledge about their natural diet is frequently lacking. In such cases we must try out various species of available plants and allow the animal to choose the most suitable food.

The amount of food given to the animal must also reflect that which is available in the natural conditions. In nature, periods of abundance alternate with periods of scarcity, and so feeding time should not be regular in the vivarium either. Periodically the animals should go without food for a couple of days. Overfed animals put on fat and their resistance to illnesses is reduced in comparison with animals that are appropriately and thoughtfully fed.

It is very important to keep the vivarium clean. The animals should regularly be supplied with fresh water and should be removed from the vivarium at least once a week to give it a thorough cleaning. In doing so, due precaution must be taken particularly in handling not only venomus snakes, but also small crocodiles and other reptiles.

Beginners should start by keeping small reptiles and amphibians native to their own country. They will spend many happy hours watching them and caring for them and will also acquire valuable experience which will allow them, eventually, to keep the rarer, more expensive and delicate species with confidence.

BIBLIOGRAPHY

Arnold, E. N. & Burton, J. A.: *A Field Guide to the Reptiles and Amphibians of Europe.* Collins, London, 1978.

Arnold, H. R.: *Provisional Atlas of the Amphibians and Reptiles of the British Isles.* Nature Conservancy Council, 1973.

Cochran, D. M.: *Living Amphibians of the World.* Doubleday & Co., New York, 1967.

Hellmich, W.: *Reptiles and Amphibians of Europe.* Blandford, London, 1964.

Leutscher, A.: *Keeping Reptiles and Amphibians.* David & Charles, Newton Abbot, 1976.

Schmidt, K. P. & Inger, R. F.: *Living Reptiles of the World.* Doubleday & Co., New York, 1962.

Smith, M. A.: *British Amphibians and Reptiles.* Collins, London, 1973 (5th edition).

Steward, J. W.: *The Snakes of Europe.* David & Charles, Newton Abbot, 1971.

Steward, J. W.: *The Tailed Amphibians of Europe.* David & Charles, Newton Abbot, 1969.

INDEX OF COMMON NAMES

INDEX OF LATIN NAMES